I Followed the Feathers

and

Found Myself

Jane McNally

BALBOA.
PRESS

A DIVISION OF HAY HOUSE

Balboa Press books may be ordered through booksellers or by contacting:

Balboa Press
A Division of Hay House
1663 Liberty Drive
Bloomington, IN 47403
www.balboapress.com
1-(877) 407-4847

Because of the dynamic nature of the Internet, any web addresses or links contained in this book may have changed since publication and may no longer be valid. The views expressed in this work are solely those of the author and do not necessarily reflect the views of the publisher, and the publisher hereby disclaims any responsibility for them.

The author of this book does not dispense medical advice or prescribe the use of any technique as a form of treatment for physical, emotional, or medical problems without the advice of a physician, either directly or indirectly. The intent of the author is only to offer information of a general nature to help you in your quest for emotional and spiritual well-being. In the event you use any of the information in this book for yourself, which is your constitutional right, the author and the publisher assume no responsibility for your actions.

Any people depicted in stock imagery provided by Thinkstock are models, and such images are being used for illustrative purposes only.
Certain stock imagery © Thinkstock.

Printed in the United States of America

ISBN: 978-1-4525-7049-5 (sc)
ISBN: 978-1-4525-7050-1 (e)
ISBN: 978-1-4525-7051-8 (hc)

Library of Congress Control Number: 2013904413

Balboa Press rev. date: 03/22/2013

Acknowledgments

I want to say a big thank you to everyone who has
crossed my path that has believed in me and my gift.
Zena and Neil Hammond my soul friends who
walk the same path as me, I love you dearly, Jamie
and Jade who I also love dearly this is for you.

Especially Buddy McNally welcome to the world

All the team at Balboa Press your great especially
Elisabeth Deiwert and Stephanie Cornthwaite
A heartfelt thank you to Glenn Harold a true
business man with integrity and an amazing healer
and Hypnotherapist as well, thank you for your kind
words of support in the process of my writing.

For Milo my lovely pet dog in spirit who opened my
heart and bought me much joy when alive.
For Amber my guardian Angel that this would
not of happened if I did not listen to her.
My granddad in spirit who watches over me thank you.
And Penny my amazing talented PA, whom
has been a star throughout this journey.
And lastly my loving Mother in spirit
love you mum and always will.

Table of Contents

Preface

BACK IN 2006 I WAS given a prompt to write this book, after a while and many questions internally like I am not a writer and other negative self-talk I gave in and so it is.

I could not ignore the messages to tell you how my life had been healed and transformed by these spiritual beings called Angels. After all their goal was to let you know that they are there for you too and through this writing I hope it will make you see that you are not alone either.

It's a strange and true journey that sounds like some sci-fi film-but oh no it is real and true.

My journey of self-love and healing is heartwarming, non-judgmental and easy to read.

It came about soon after my mum's death because her dying awoke me even more to realise my dream and get the information and guidance out to many who feels they need help or healing. I was alone after being separated from my husband and in a place of deep pain and transformation mourning two losses I found strength from within to make my life worth living after all I had been through life was not going to get me down.. I had been in co-dependency relationships for most of my adult life. Now it was my time to be the person I wanted to be and to be a mentor-guide for others that have had such situations and needed to find their truth and themselves.

I feel more passionately about healing than ever before, my guides have channeled much in the way of Healing meditation's to use on my clients and also myself, I have seen Miracles happen and people be healed with my gift I am in Awe of the power within and the fact I have been chosen to be the channel is a true Honor, I won't give up on people especially Children whom I feel for as they are the innocent ones and I want to help where I can to save them from pain it can take a long time to recover from abusive relationships and dysfunctional upbringings.

I have become more spontaneous, embraced my femininity and learned new skills and lessons along the way about boundaries and self-love, I have grown beyond belief and feel so light and carry so much light I struggle with low energies as my consciousness has changed to that of love and peace that's my language My universal truth "I AM" presence has taken over much to my delight.

After all my soul chose these lessons in life and there is nothing we can do to change that, but be grateful that Healers exist to help us on our journey, I have had many healings and guidance before turning professional and I am grateful for those that helped me in my time of need such as the Spiritual workers at Kingston Spiritual Church for without them I don't know where I would be now.

I am proud to be a part of the Change going on right now on Earth and hope to help many more on this Journey, I have met many people personally and talked nonstop over the internet and telephone globally

I thank you for choosing me as your healer and showing me love and support also after all it is about giving and receiving and energy flow.

Many of you have written to me, saying how much I have helped you, well remember it's the Angels not me that made you find me so thank them as well.

Jane McNally

Introduction

EVER SINCE I WAS A child I have always wanted to be free to be in the world to see it through my eyes in my way and to experience life as I have wanted, to explore this idea or that option to see where it lead me.

Unknown to me at the time I was born as what is known as a "Star Child", that is, one who comes to this earth to teach love, self-expression and spiritual growth. Curiously, I have often been called an "earth angel" by many people – that is an angel but without wings.

I grew up in a conventional household with my family, but I was different for I had a gift and it was this that led me down many different routes. At times it almost freaked me out for I came across much in the way of spiritual phenomena. At one stage I ran away in the opposite direction for there was no way that I wanted to travel that path.

What the spirit had planned for me was quite different. Initially I didn't always trust what was in store for I often couldn't believe what my senses were telling me. It felt frightening when I first started communicating with higher beings (the angels) and I was in some awe of it all, but I needed the evidence some proof if I were to act in an ambassadorial role for them. I got that all right in all shapes and sizes.

This book is about my journey of self-discovery of my true spirit and how much help is available to us if we only learn how, and perhaps who we should ask.

When I discovered the angels I promised them I would work for them because, quite simply, I then realised that they had been with me all the time and they still are. I sacrificed my home and a secure income to be where I am today but I am happier far beyond monetary means because what I have is precious - and no money can match that.

A true sense of being looked after, a sense of peace and that all is well. .

I have always been fascinated by parapsychology and, when I started getting messages from ascended masters and loved ones in spirit I must tell you that if you don't listen then these beings shout all the louder until you do but always with your interests at heart.

I have and still am happy to have risked all to stand up for what I believe to be an after-life or an existence beyond this physical one. If I had been asked that when I was about twenty years old or so then perhaps I might not have been so ready but as I have had all these wonderful things happen to me and I now know why. It was to be able to help others, the sceptics of this world - call them what you will, the non-believers who fail to see the truth in that our consciousness exists whether we are alive or not.

The angels and other loved ones in spirit work with us via a kind of telepathy relaying messages of their existence to us earth-bound mortals to explain it all. Part of this is through what we term medium-ship or the passing of messages to people. Often, such messages were to people I have never met before and came from mothers and fathers who have passed on but who gave their names freely and who spoke of how they died and where they lived. I could not possibly have known this information just by sitting next to a possible relative or even talking to them at end of a telephone line.

I prefer to work with the higher energies because my purpose here is to teach about the angels and spiritual growth. I also heal people as a channel. The encounters with angels have been documented by writers all over the world. Films have been made and these matters are now beginning to filter out into the world of the theatre and the arts.

In these rather material times more and more people are beginning to come out of the spiritual closet to tell of their experiences. I am proud to be one of those who have a story to tell of how my life has been changed so dramatically although it did take a while to get me to listen.

This book is about how I was awakened from my ordinary, everyday life into one filled with the magic that only love, peace and that special feeling of protection can bring. All that I have written about here is true revelation of all that has happened to me since I was a child.

Some of it felt a tad unpleasant at the time and it was certainly awesome in places. But, the main point is that I show here that we are loved and protected beyond normal belief.

If you are ready to be aware of this and if you can open your heart and mind to receive messages for you to follow than come and see for yourself, listen and enjoy.

PART ONE

The Spiritual Nudges

CHAPTER ONE
My Early Years

IN THE EARLY NINETEEN SIXTIES I was born into a London based working class family although, to be sure, my life was never going to be ordinary. However, I was not going to find out until my mid-twenties precisely what was in store for me.

The family lived in Pimlico London, nice and close to the West-end for most things. Our parents raised Suzy, Stephen and I me as best they could on their wages. It was not a bad childhood really, for we lived in a three bedroom maisonette and I had to share a bedroom with my sister. As I recall it had pink woodchip wallpaper and mostly plywood furniture. My brother had his own room and I never really felt that interested to go in or explore it.

Father loved to collect swords and animal heads which tended to hang on the wall. As I recall there was always a deer head on the stairs. This meant I had to pass it regularly which was not a great help. I was, of course, a sensitive and to pass by it so often really scared me. It wouldn't surprise to think that it was this that may well have made me choose to be a vegetarian these days.

While my father, who worked at BAC as an engineer for most of my younger days, our mother worked part time in a local factory and, somehow, always managed to be there with us at home where she really did make a splendid job of looking after her brood.

Neither of my parents was overly religious or even spiritually inclined for that matter but they always made us attend Sunday school at our local church, St Gabriel's. I have often mused over this and, being practical as well, perhaps it was her way of getting a rest from looking after us. I know that it was here that I got a "sense" of God. Alas, quite a few friends made fun of me and I was known as a "weirdo" locally. Curiously, it didn't really bother me then or even today, for that matter.

My first proper "spirit" encounter occurred when I was eight and this was to be the start of my journey into all things supernatural, spiritual and angelic.

One evening as my mother tucked me and my sister into bed, she switched the light off in her usual manner. Despite it having been quite an ordinary day and evening I remember that I had woken suddenly at about 4am and saw what seemed to be an elderly lady standing by my bed.

I just screamed, ripped off the bedclothes and ran sobbing, absolutely terrified, into my parent's bedroom where I knew I would be safe. I know I blurted out what I thought had happened and my mother who was by now wide awake did her best to calm me down.

It was bitterly disappointing to my young mind that neither parent really believed me but they allowed me to stay safe and warm in their bed for the rest of the night. As I had made up my mind I wasn't going back to my own bed I just squeezed down between them and tried to re-settle myself into some semblance of rest, and hopefully, sleep for the rest of the night.

The following night I remembered sliding warily into my bed and huddled as tight as I could against the wall with my head under the bedclothes. I also remembered thinking that, if I were to waken during the night, the last thing I was going to do was look around the room - for anything!

It was getting somewhere near my tenth birthday and mum and dad were planning our holiday. As dad was always up for adventure for he loved to explore places wherever we stayed we spent many a happy time camping out. Often, we would go to Spain and that meant dad would bring home a trophy of some kind – once it was bulls' head. At other times it would have been something equally as weird again.

Shortly after this holiday I began my secondary school education locally.

Now this was a new adventure!

It was a fairly new building and had only been open for about five years. In many ways it seemed to me to look like a giant greenhouse because it was apparently created with 80% glass in its overall make-up. Both my brother and my sister had attended here but were nearing the end of their time there when it became my turn for an education here.

This new school made me feel rather uneasy because I have always liked to spend time on my own but despite this I soon settled in and made one or two nice friends. We would hang out together just to have fun much as most girls or boys of this age did and still do apparently.

However, it soon became a tad difficult for me as I seemed to be unable to settle down at lesson times. I found it hard to concentrate like the others and I seemed to be day-dreaming all the time. I had little or no interest in things like history for example. It was as if I knew about such things already as if I had been here before. Further, I became so sensitive to these energies around me I needed to get away from the noise and interference all the time.

Then I found out that one or two of the girls with whom I had made friends turned out to be bullies. I am still not sure quite what was wrong but I began to stay away from school and became a regular truant.

Actually, as I didn't seem to be learning much anyway being unable to focus or absorb knowledge properly it seemed to be the best thing to do. Soon, my mother began to receive letters from the school in respect of my continuing absences.

So, when she did confront me with all this activity I really had no choice so I confessed.

She went to the school to complain but this made matters worse and anyway I kept skipping lessons.

Eventually mother was called into a meeting where she was told, in no uncertain terms, precisely what they intended to do with me.

She was informed that I was on report for continuous truant behavioural patterns. I felt that I was being punished for running away from my tormentors so I didn't care much that I had been labelled rebellious so I just kept away from school.

One day well into my third year the headmaster had me transferred into a secure unit within the school with other truants and, for my own protection, I had to go daily. On arrival we were locked in every morning so that, to me at any rate, school became a prison and also a place from where I couldn't escape.

Both of my parents were quite cross at this and my mother made a strong point of complaining but, curiously, made no attempt at having me change schools. This was probably because the school was just across the road and far too convenient really. So, I continued at the school working hard every day and with the added ignominy of being escorted home by a teacher.

So my school-days were rather fearful and more than just unpleasant. I did feel different from the other girls but was probably too young to understand it all because of my age. I was allocated to a counsellor who was supposed to help me to get over the trauma of being bullied. Even in those days I was such a sensitive soul and couldn't understand why people would be so harsh to one another.

The rest of my teenage years were equally as troubled but for different reasons. Even so, writing this has proved to be cathartic. Mum found out dad was having an affair and they split after being together for some eighteen 18 years. This was a devastating blow to the family which to all and sundry on the outside seemed happy, but in reality was not. I remember that I so often cried myself to sleep at nights while dad was gone. It was almost like bereavement at times in that I tried to comfort mum as best as I could, If nothing else came of it over the time mother and I grew much closer and more understanding of each other although my father had disappeared to make a new life with his new partner.

We were not to see him for some time and this was awful for me. Eventually, Suzy and Stephen and I met up with him again but he didn't say much. He took us on day-trip to Battersea Park where we all made the most if. We did think he might have thought we had got over it, but this was not so at all. The pain of all this stayed for many years.

At the tender age of fifteen I became involved with my first boyfriend, Ron. He lived across the river from us in Vauxhall. He was a bit of a rogue but in his own fashion he loved me – so he said. Because of this I turned a blind eye to his behaviour because it was so nice to be loved. In fact, on reflection when I look back it is now obvious to me that he had replaced my father's affections and filled this now rather large but empty void. My insecurities got the better of me and I stayed with Ron probably because of this.

Of course, I was too young to be serious with anyone and mum disapproved of him for she so often tried to tell me that he was no good, but I just carried on seeing him. He treated me badly, even cheated on me but I didn't care - I just wanted what love there was going. My self esteem was at rock bottom.

Eventually, after some five or so years together we got married and, after a little while, my son, Jamie was born, Ron let us both down and left us to be with another women. In essence, it was like my father's activities all over again.

It was at this time I started to become interested in astrology, horoscopes and all that study entails. Perhaps a glimpse into the future was what I needed right then. Actually, this interest did rather become something of an addiction for I would read everything astrologically that I could find just to get some hope or an idea for myself as to what my future had in store.

CHAPTER TWO

My Mother And The Medium

OUR FAVOURITE UNCLE FREDERICK WAS my mother's only brother. Actually, he was our only uncle because he was the only male of his generation being the only boy along with six girls! It never seemed to worry him too much; he got along with them all as far as we knew. He adored his mother who we knew as Nan Lucy. She had lost her husband in the Second World War after all her children had been born and brought them up on her own. She was one very special lady to not only her own children but to her grandchildren as well.

Now my uncle Fred was quite a sensitive soul as well. Few knew of how much so partly because he kept this side of his life very much to himself. I was to find this out for myself when I went with my mother to visit him at a psychiatric hospital somewhere in Kent. He was being treated in a ward for people with mental health problems as he was having strange things going on in his mind.

He was being treated by a doctor who was doing his best to try to sort out exactly what my uncle was experiencing. He had been complaining that he was worried and a little fearful of seeing people from the spirit world. In those days doctors were more than sceptical about such things and were a little unsure of how they should treat him.

Once my uncle Fred was eventually released he came home and took up his normal life. He worked at the local Town Hall as a dustman which enabled him to look after his wife and three children in reasonable comfort.

However, although he travelled fairly extensively around the borough because of his work and his private interests many people thought he was a normal every day sort of chap – but the inner man was still seriously troubled. Whatever it was came to a head one August when he took an overdose of tablets and drank a bottle of bleach.

Just prior to this last act he had told one of my aunts that he had seen the spirit of one of his late friends in his local social club. This seemed to have been the last straw for he couldn't cope with the physical loss of who had been a good close friend. He missed him a lot and, in the end, it all got too much for him. His funeral took place in Streatham and because she was rather old and frail Nanny Lee wasn't told of what has happened for some time.

The years began to pass and I was living in Victoria with Jamie, my son aged 8 and I was juggling being a mother and being a student working toward my food and nutrition exams. The father of my child never really bothered too much with us but which did rather add to my responsibilities quite a bit but we were happy and we managed.

Then, out of the blue, just when I was still quite young and naive, Nanny Lee was taken into hospital with bronchitis. Her conditioned worsened and she passed away aged ninety-three. Her funeral was enormous for she was great local personality who had raised a lot of money for various charities.

Her cortege consisted of twenty seven cars and she had a police escort all the way from Pimlico to Streatham where we celebrated her long and active life at St Saviour's church. All funerals are poignant one way or another but she had been one very special lady – someone I will never forget. It was more or less left up to me to fuss around my mother after this and I was happy to do what I could with the rest of the family doing their best as and when they could, of course.

Not long after my grandmother passed on my mother mentioned that she was going to see a Mrs Ann Blake who was a medium. Mother explained what a medium was and does and suggested I might like to go along with her. I became quite intrigued for this was my very first experience of things supernatural, that is, apart from my interest in horoscopes and astrology. I agreed to go for I wanted to experience just exactly what was what.

We arrived at the lady's West-end address a little before our afternoon appointment time. By now I had learned that this lady was famous for her "readings" of celebrities like Meg Richardson from the old midlands television programme Crossroads and other equally well known people.

We went in by the front door through the hall and up the stairs to the first floor. The decor struck me as we went for I noticed the rather unusual wallpaper. It was rather bright and full of flowers and certainly not to my taste, I thought silently. Ann Blake met us and led us into a small waiting room full of pictures of celebrities.

Mum was hoping to get a message from her mother and, just as I thought Ann Blake was about to start her work she ushered mum and herself into a separate room while I was left to mull over the many and varied books on Spiritualism in Ann's library. I sat there feeling a little nervous as to what was happening and another feeling, this time of some trepidation washed over me, I would love to have known my grandmother was well and alive in spirit. I also thought that this whole exercise was a way of testing my beliefs following on from what I had and was being taught in church.

Eventually, after what seemed to be a very long time, my mother finally emerged from the room with a smile that was almost a beam on her face now that was good to see, something had obviously gone very well. I was so pleased for little of any real worth had been that good of late. But it looked as though Ann Blake had changed all that into something really positive was going well.

It was now my turn to have a private consultation with Mrs Blake. As I went into the room my mother went outside for some fresh air and to digest all that she just learned. As I sat down I got out my pad and pencil to take notes when Ann Blake told me it wasn't necessary and indicated the small tape recorder already switched on and running discreetly placed on a side table. While I waited for her to begin my eyes just couldn't resist scanning over all the celebrities in the photographs on the sideboard, the tables and on the walls.

My body tension began to increase quite significantly as I waited for Ann Blake to begin the session.

I tried as hard as I could to sink back and relax in the green velour sofa as Ann began to talk. She covered so much ground in what seemed such a short time. What she knew about me and what I had been through was astounding. And how she contacted my beloved grandmother who spoke of something only she and I knew about will always stay in my memory.

She referred to a garnet brooch that I had been given as a keepsake and this along with the mention of other gifts and events together with other matters. To be with Ann Blake was simply an absolute joy for she was such a mine of information.

After my time with Ann Blake I went and found my mother who was still in the garden and we hurried off home for we both wanted to listen not only to each other's readings but also to hear own again.

To hear again the evidence of my grandmother talking to me raised so many questions as to how one person could glean so much information about a deceased third party amazed me.

Following on from this first interview with Ann Blake I became more and more intrigued by the afterlife and began to attend more Psychic Fairs and similar events. I was thirsty for more knowledge in respect of the spiritualistic nature and aspects of such matters. In fact, this became so much this was to be a turning point in my life.

I spent more time visiting Spiritualist churches especially the Kingston-Upon-Thames Spiritualist church for I felt that this special place was where I was first drawn to the most. I went on many evenings and tried to get there on the Sundays as well. Often, as I sat in among the congregation I hoped I might get another message from my late grandmother. Although this did not come to pass I was totally struck and often just plain amazed at the fascinating accuracy of some of the Mediums who were either a part of the church or who were specially invited visitors.

Spiritualist Churches always seemed to be such friendly places. There were always such equally friendly people who would set your mind at rest and who could organise Psychic Fairs and events with such a consummate ease. I had so many questions to ask and even as I got the answers it would raise other issues. All these were gradually answered and, as the time drew on, I became more and more at ease. Not only this but my knowledge of psychic matters increased tremendously because of the care and thoughtfulness these people engendered became.

I remember at about this time that I told my mother of my desire to increase my experience of the psychic world and of how fascinated it made me. I also remember that shortly after this I had purchased a pack of Tarot Cards as well as a set of Angel Cards. I used to look at and study them a lot at the beginning until one day my mother found me involved in a session with them.

I was quite stunned when she severely admonished me and asked me not to dabble in such things. If nothing else, this was a bit hypocritical to say the least for she was still having reasonably regular sessions with Ann Blake. This time it was me who turned a blind eye to such advice and I continued to follow my curiosity.

CHAPTER THREE

The Spirit Visits

SHORTLY AFTER MY VISITS TO Ann Blake, I became more interested in visiting Psychic Fairs and having psychic readings performed for me. This, along with other experiences, has now made me become absolutely intrigued by the entire paranormal world – anything from psychic phenomena through to the fascinating spheres of astrology and all that it entails.

I happened to be visiting my sister Suzy, who was then living in Worcester Park on the borders of south London and north Surrey, she said that there was a local Psychic Fair in a nearby public house. It was she who made the suggestion that we might go along for a short visit, just to see what was going on. So, after a short walk we arrived at the venue, paid a minimal entrance fee, and entered the main hall.

Although it was now something like eight o'clock on a Wednesday evening the place was solid with people all making their way around the many stalls, many of which resembled an Aladdin's Cave of crystals, colourful clothing, incense, books and a multitude of all kinds of paraphernalia one could not normally buy in any old ordinary shop along the high street. It was mesmerising and absorbing; so much so, I felt I really belonged here.

As we slowly made our way around the stalls, looking at this and that, taking it all in, more or less just feeling at home I came across a book stall and had to have a rummage. One of the many tomes for sale was one on Angels and I had to buy it on the spot. My love of reading and my ever widening interest in this strange world of new thinking and beliefs was fast getting the better of me. I knew I was going to make a cup of tea and snuggle up with the book later on that night.

The next major event of my visit here was a meeting with a lady psychic clairvoyant who called herself Rosemarie. She agreed to give me a reading later as she was fairly heavily booked up and, as we had some time to spare Suzy and I wandered off to have a coffee and a light snack in the small refreshment area. Afterwards, Suzy went off on her own while I made my way back to the lady clairvoyant.

Given my experience with Ann Blake a little while earlier I felt a tad unsure of myself as I made my way gingerly toward Rosemarie's booth. In essence this would be my first paid visit to a clairvoyant off my own back – I just didn't know what to expect at all.

I sat at the little table opposite and noted her lovely red hair and almost glowing skin which was beautifully set off by a stunning necklace. Because I had expected something (or someone) completely different to her I felt somewhat off-balance. I had always thought that psychics dressed to meet the part but this was one very ordinary looking lady, and she had charisma too. This was no obviously pseudo witch or gypsy; this lady was normal.

Of course, her table was a little cluttered with all the tools of her calling or trade with items like candles, crystals and tarot cards. But, quite out of the ordinary was small tape recorder with a crystal ball sitting on it over a violet cloth. It was what one has come to expect I suppose when one visits such people. It all helped to portray her work with that little added air of mystery.

Introductions over, she began her reading. I just sat and listened nodding or shaking my head here and there if she hit on something which was right. She was my idea of a good psychic, someone who just talked and didn't ask too many questions.

When my time was up I felt blown away by her accuracy. It had been spot on through-out. She went on to give me her address should I ever want to have another reading at any time in the future. Well, if anyone ought to know she would know if I would be back for more, wouldn't she?

For the fee I paid I also received a tape recording of my session to take with me – something I could listen to over and over again at a later time. I was so pleased with what and how she had demonstrated her art I kept in touch. Later, I eventually began to learn a system of reading and understanding Tarot Cards with her when I started to visit her home in Epsom in Surrey on a regular basis. It was during the course of all this that we also became good friends.

By this time Suzy had caught up with me and was ready to leave. This was fair for she had been musing around and seen and done all she wanted to while waiting for me to finish. So, off we went to her home where I stayed that night and then travelled home the next morning. .

When I arrived home I collected Jamie from my mother's house and we went home for the evening, I prepared our evening meal as usual after which we watched some TV cuddled up on the sofa. I put him to bed at his usual time, tucked him up and said goodnight.

I continued to watch some TV until about ten-thirty or so and decided to go to bed – it had been a long day and I felt pleasantly tired. As a rule, I like to read a before going to sleep so, after making my usual cocoa, I threw back the duvet, switched on the bedside light and began to indulge myself in my new book.

It was not long before my eyelids began to droop and, as I felt even more tired, just before I succumbed I remembered to switch off the light, got comfortable and lay my head on my pillow, closed my eyes and drifted off....

Something woke me – I don't know what is was but I remember quite clearly being awakened, I thought by voices. I thought I had heard two people speaking almost as if were the radio but that was switched off so it could not have been on there. In any case the conversation seemed to be so swift between the speakers that what was being said hardly made sense. While still slightly bemused my head began to feel very heavy and then almost as slowly so did the rest of my body and I lay there, frightened and virtually paralysed.

At first I felt as though I was stuck to the bed but then realised that I was floating out of my body and that I could see it (me) laying on the bed below me. Then one minute I crashed to the floor and, just as quickly, I found myself floating up in the air again. After a couple of minutes of this (it may have been a lot more, of course, but I really wasn't sure of time at all at this moment in time), I just as quickly found myself back in my body again. As soon as I regained the use of my body I sat bolt upright and switched on the light again.

Now – was it a dream or was it real? I really didn't know anything for sure in those first few minutes as struggled to get my mind working properly again but one thing was for sure, I didn't like it very much at all. The more I thought about it or tried to conceive an idea that would hold water I found another thought to work on and, in this rather confused state I must have fallen asleep

The next morning after I had taken Jamie to school I made my way over to my mother's place and, over a cup of tea I began to relate all that had taken place the night before. I had expected some sympathy or at least a kind word that might have helped. Instead, she dismissed the whole episode and from her tone it was evident she was thinking that whatever had happened to uncle Fred now seemed to be starting to happen to me.

Despite mum's attitude and general demeanour I thought it best to let things drop there and, for the rest of the time carried on as though it were a normal time. However, as bedtime drew ever nearer I did begin to get quite apprehensive although I tried not show it. When the time came the main concession was to go to sleep with the light on - just in case!

But it was not to be. As I put my head on the pillow it began to feel as though it were burning and this feeling swept down my body until, once again, I felt as though I couldn't move even if I wanted to. I was, to all intents and purposes paralysed for a second time. And, again, I began to experience a floating feeling as rose toward the ceiling and moving from side to side and up and down. I seemed to have no control over my body at all for I could see it lying flat on the bed far below me. I was shocked scared and frightened.

Of course, this time, the light was on so I felt a little better, not much, I'll agree, but it was better than being totally in the dark like the previous night. I could hear the voices again as well. Two people consistently talking to and at each other. It was like having visitors only I couldn't see them. The heaviness gradually eased and as I opened my eyes again I noted the time to be just past eleven o'clock. I went straight to my phone and dialled my mother's number.

Unfortunately, in the light of what I had been experiencing I really had no idea as to how she would react but I soon found out. I apologised for the time and tried to tell her what had been happening. She half listened but was of no real help although she did try to do her best to calm me down. This time, however, she did ask for reassurance about Jamie after I had told her that he was alright she eased back a tad and said we should talk about it all in the morning. I went back and lay on the bed half anticipating another episode but nothing happened and I must have drifted off to wake at about seven the next morning.

My mother was of very little help when I visited her later on that next morning. She seemed bemused and was fairly dismissive of the whole affair. No matter what I said or tried to get over to her was of little use. To her it was mostly a lot of nonsense.

As the days went past the strange experiences I was having began to get the better of me and, on one occasion I telephoned my mother at about one in the morning crying down the phone. She arranged to call a taxi for me and Jamie and while I was getting him ready I said that nanny wasn't feeling too well and that we had to go to see her. Almost immediately we arrived I felt fine, relaxed and at peace. That night and we slept like a log.

The next day I took Jamie back to school after which I made a phone call to my local Spiritualist Church to seek some advice and guidance. We went over all that was taking place and they told me that either I needed the help of a trained Spirit release specialist or, if things were worse, then a priest might be necessary to exorcise the house.

My mother, however, wasn't so sure and she suggested that I make arrangements to get in touch with my local GP, Doctor Winkler, to see if he could help. So I called him and made an appointment wondering if he would understand once I had explained all my troubles to him.

CHAPTER FOUR

The Psychiatric Hospital

IT WAS NEARLY FOUR O'CLOCK by the time I arrived at the doctor's surgery and I walked hesitantly through the narrow passage that lead to the receptionist.

"Hello Jane, my dear. Take a seat," she said.

This was making me more nervous by the minute and I was wondering how he would take the news that I was hearing voices and floating outside of my body.

"Um," I thought as I entered Doctor Winkler's surgery, "Bet he hasn't had one like this for a while!"

I sat on the old chair, looked at my old doctor and remembered that he had known me since I was a baby. However, I was still a little unsure he was unprepared for my visit today. I began to feel rather embarrassed and lowered my head.

He smiled, "Hello Jane, what seems to be the problem?"

"Well, er, actually doctor, you see..."

I began to explain about the out-of-body experiences I was having; of how I was floating around the room for the last six weeks or so at home and also that I was hearing voices.

He looked me in the eye, took hold of my hand and said gently, "Now listen. Now don't worry, you have been very brave to come in and tell me about all this".

He paused for a moment. "I am going to give you a letter to take to the Westminster hospital.

"Why?" I asked, still feeling rather sorry for myself.

"They will be able help you find out why this is happening. You'll be fine - and don't worry; they'll want to make a few observations so trust them."

I trusted Doctor Winkler immensely for he had been our family physician for many years so I waited while he wrote out the note and took the little brown envelope from him.

When I left the surgery I decided to go straight to the hospital.

When I got there I was kept in the general waiting area for a little and then a sister who seemed to have appeared from nowhere smiled pleasantly at me.

"Would you like to come with me please"?

We passed through a few corridors where we entered a little office and I gave her the letter from my GP.

As she took it she said, "Doctor Winkler has given me an outline over the phone about what seems to have been happening and we would like you to stay with us for a little while so that we may carry out a few tests and see what the problem or problems might be."

To say I was a little unprepared for this was an understatement.

I wasn't sure what to do or how to react about staying in the hospital. After all, the notice over the door did say that this was the psychiatric wing. I was sure I was all right; I felt ok and hadn't thought for a moment that I might have a mental health problem. Well, not yet anyway!

The kindly sister took me from her office into a small ward, showed me to a bed and left me alone with my thoughts. Suddenly, the starkness of the place hit me hard. The whole place had an air of gloom and there was a strong smell of disinfectant that seemed to have been used on everything.

There were four beds in the room, two to my left and on the one next to me a rather thin young girl sat on the edge. I said hello but did not hear a reply. It was sad to see the way she looked. I had a feeling she might have been suffering from anorexia and, as she was obviously in a world all her own I felt that if she wanted to talk, she would.

So, here I was, in a psychiatric ward with an anorexic girl, plain bare walls, hardly any furniture and no blinds to block out the daylight.

A robe was lying at the end of my bed which I put it into the locker so I knew where to find it later. Then it struck me that I ought to let my mother know what was happening so I began to look for a phone to let her know where I was and what was going on.

I found a payphone on wheels in one of the corridors, pushed it to a place for some privacy and dialled her number.

Her response was typical and it took me some time to calm her down. In retrospect I suppose one should have understood how she must have felt. Eventually, she calmed down, agreed to look after Jamie and we agreed to talk more in the morning.

I made my way back to the ward and sat bored and a little lonely on the hard bed, not knowing what to do with myself. A cup of tea is the usual universal panacea at such times so I gathered myself together again and began to look for the canteen.

The journey was a faintly eerie one because I felt that I was being starred at with eyes burrowing into my back. I felt different, as if I didn't belong here. In the canteen there were many people, some in robes and a few in outdoor wear. The thought passed through my head that I was in a scene from "One Flew over the Cuckoo's Nest" and I felt scary thinking that some of these people were perhaps having the same experiences as me.

I remember that there was an actress from the "Carry-On" films who looked depressed, which may well have been the reason she was in there in the first place.

I thought long and hard over my cup of tea and then made my way back to my little ward. On the way I noticed some doors had bars on them and I wondered idly who or what was behind them. I suppose I must have felt a little fearful for my safety in the place so when I reached the room I was pleased to see the girl was still there.

At least I had some company.

I changed into the night-clothes, wished my room-mate goodnight, laid down on the bed and began to doze off.

As I began to drift away I thought I heard a snake hissing in my ear and then I saw one on the floor. I remember jumping up and called for help. The duty nurse came to my aid quickly and did her best to calm me down but I was half-hysterical and demanded to speak to my mother. I still can't remember exactly what the nurse said or did but she gave me a pill, led me back to the room, put me to bed where I must have floated off to sleep quite quickly.

The sun was streaming through the windows on to the bed when I woke suddenly. The clock said it was seven o'clock as I came to and then the experiences from the night before came rushing back to me and I sat up quickly.

Quite what happened in the next half an hour or so didn't really register except that the nurse who came in helped me get ready for the day and brought me breakfast saying that I should have it in the ward. She also told me that I would be seen later in the morning by the duty doctor and that she would come back to take me there. In the meantime she suggested I stay in the ward and listen to the radio or read while I waited.

At about eleven o'clock she came back for me and we went through the maze of corridors (I never ever got used to how many there were while I was in there) and we went into a fairly large room where there were about twenty or so people present.

The oldest one there was a doctor who made sure I felt at home and not fazed by so many people – all of whom were students apparently.

Suddenly, we were discussing what was happening to me. The doctor explained that I was having a form of hypnogenic sleep. This can (and does) happen when you put your head on the pillow and the blood rushes to the head. Some people are inclined to hallucinate while others experience nothing at all. He thought that I needed to take tranquillisers to help calm my mind and for me to come back in about a month after being released.

I was convinced I was having paranormal experiences but was quite unable to explain. What I did say was dismissed. However, he was a kindly man and made sure that I would do as he asked so I really had very little choice then but to do as he suggested.

I was taken back to my ward where I changed into my out-door clothes. Then I was taken to the pharmacy to get the doctor's prescription and from there I was allowed to go home. Pleased at not having to stay in the hospital for another night and being home again was good. The tablets went into the medicine cabinet and eventually I disposed of them.

It was around this time I began to think I should visit my local Spiritual church as I believed I was still having Spirit experiences. I made an appointment to meet with a healer at Kingston Spiritualist church.

It was two days after I left the hospital when I got to see Joan - a healer and medium. She took me to an office at the back of the large hall where we sat down and chatted for a long time. I told her the whole story from the beginning to the present time.

At last, I had now met with someone who understood what might be going on for she felt that I was "open" to the spirit world and needed to know much more about it.

She arranged for me to take some special exercises that she explained would protect me from negative energies and keep me protected.

She also wanted me to see a healer who was good at releasing "attachments" and, as he worked from home she gave me his number.

I telephoned him and made an appointment to meet him at his home in Walton-on-Thames.

When we met I noticed somehow that Ray had a lovely aura around him. He told me he worked with his son who was now in the spirit world.

Ray had a warm and comfortable room kept especially for healing. It was here that I received Reiki on his couch to enable negative spirit energies to leave me alone.

I remember feeling Ice cold like a corpse and it was very strange experience to say the least.

When this was over Ray told me of another spirit who appeared but that this one was a guide. All this was happening rather too fast for me to keep up with and was a trifle scary if I were to be honest. However, the really good news was that Ray said that he had removed a negative energy from my aura. He further explained some of the tasks that I had to maintain to keep my chakras "clean", free and protected from further interference.

He went on to say that he would help further in order for me to contact and accept more spirit help from my guide (or angel). He further stated that once all the right connections had been made it was expected that I would make a good healer because of my strong sensitivity to such things.

When I left Ray I felt a lot better and much clearer in my mind about what was happening to me and that my future life would be really worthwhile.

CHAPTER FIVE

Hazel And The Baptist Church

HAZEL, A FRIEND OF MY sister, was someone we often used to visit at her rather sumptuous home in Berkshire. She was a small woman married to her larger-than-life husband, Nigel, who was heavily involved in the pop music industry. Suzy, my sister, and I often used to go to Hazel's to chat over some of the old times of when she and Hazel worked together in the music business and, of course, to bring ourselves up to date with what we were all up to at the time.

Hazel spent much time reading the bible for she was interested in the church quite a lot. She was deeply convinced that God had helped her work out problems. I felt she was quite lonely as Nigel spent a lot of time away from their home in his promotion work. They had two lovely children, Tom and Alice and, while they took up a lot of her time and she may have seemed happy on the surface, I felt that inwardly she was very lonely really deep down.

On one trip to her home she created a super lunch and we sat chatting in her lovely dining room overlooking the river. Curiously, it was at times like these I often wondered if someone famous had sat where I was now sitting. We had begun to talk about spiritual and religious issues when she half changed the subject and started to speak of Nigel and his illness. Apparently, he had contracted multiple sclerosis but, she alleged, he had been cured by someone from their church.

Hazel claimed that their local vicar had called on them once or twice and that one day he had begun a healing process. He had placed his hands on Nigel, and started to speak gently in a language she did not understand and, despite he (Nigel) being a non-believer the cleric seemed to have been responsible of curing him of that terrible crippling disease.

After she had related this story it felt normal to tell her of the out-of-the-body experiences that I had been enduring. She recommended that I should pray and meditate for then God would help me. This advice really changed my life for the better for while I was not aware of meditation then I did believe in God and had done so since I was a little girl but had never really known why.

She gave me a copy of the New Testament and suggested that I should read it when I felt that I should. Now at that time it was not on my mind to go to church or read the bible as I felt it a bit of a bore and although she always spoke of how much fun she had had at church somehow it just did not seem to be for me.

But, I was willing to give it a try so, when I got home that evening I had a quick search around and, once I had found a suitable spot, which eventually proved to be my bedroom, I had a light clean-up and was soon ready to proceed.

I lit a candle, sat on my bed, rested my head against the soft headboard and tried to calm myself; an undertaking that rather proved to be like trying to squeeze cement from a tube of tooth-paste. Because my mind was always very busy, the challenge of meditation was going to prove to be a hard business. Nevertheless,

I closed my eyes and that was it; my thoughts seemed to speed up as all sorts of issues flew past: shopping lists, school runs, visits to my mother, birthdays - you name it, and it came into my mind.

I remembered that Hazel had said that I was just to let go but this was no easy task. On this first occasion my thoughts did eventually begin to slow up and, as they did so, a feeling of contentment and relaxation began to flow over me. My body began to feel a lot lighter and the ensuing weightlessness and calm was peaceful and all-pervading. Eventually, I found that I had actually managed to stay still for a whole half-an-hour or so and that, mentally at any rate I could give myself a pat on the back for getting thus far.

As the weeks passed I practised more and more meditation until one day while in my lounge a huge feeling of peace washed over me as I was going about my daily tasks. I felt so serene and happy I was sure that an angel or other spiritual presence had come close to me. Alas, this lovely moment did not last long but while it was with me it was lovely and I really wanted it to stay forever.

Meditation was beginning to take a hold on me so I decided to read about it more and perhaps, see if there were any books that might be of some help. I wanted to find out more, to understand what might be possible and, of course, the obvious benefits and meaning behind it all.

I came across a phrase that implied meditation brings about a deep inner tranquillity that is both so relaxing and revitalising it helps to dissolve stress and fatigue. Further, it also serves to promote happiness, health, creativity and clear thinking to such an extent that it raises our consciousness to a level of unlimited potential within us.

The weeks and months began to gather speed as they seemed to fly past and I began getting ideas to go to church. Inwardly, I was sure that this would be good for me but I was unable to fully understand or even comprehend why I should want to go. These feelings grew steadily stronger and, so one day I found myself heading to my local Baptist church in Cheam.

I was greeted by a little Chinese lady who offered me a bible for the service which was about to begin. I sat down on one of the benches with some of the other people present and soon became caught up in the proceedings listening to the vicar give his sermon and say prayers for the sick. A short while afterward he had us all up on our feet singing and clapping. I must admit I found it most quite enjoyable and thoroughly enjoyed the feeling of the uplifting energy that had swept through my body. I was also rather surprised at the power and difference that this morning's first worship had brought to me.

When the service was over we all went down stairs where tea, coffee and, of course, biscuits were served. While standing with my cup and all on my own I felt a little lost because everyone seemed to know everybody else when I spotted the little Chinese lady making her way toward me.

She introduced herself as Mrs Wing and we began to chat almost like old friends. She certainly had a way of getting me to open up for I found myself telling her why I was there, about Hazel and all the other issues that I had been thinking about. She offered to visit me at home and I agreed because her nature really interested me. After all that had been going on in my life I was going through a bit of a rough patch and wanted some guidance. I needed a kind ear to listen and I looked forward to her first visit.

Mrs Wing arrived a few days later in the early afternoon and I made tea as one does and we sat and began to talk. We covered so much in the first few hours it was astonishing but I warmed to this lady who was so attentive, kindly and appreciative of what was happening to me. After I had spoken for some time she began to talk to me about God and how He would help me. She was one very strong, determined personality, a lovely lady and so full of her faith.

During the course of our chat in which we discussed so many different subjects she did vehemently and very strongly advise me against the use of the tarot cards. She was of the opinion that they were the Devil's work and that no one, especially me, should touch them. While I tried to digest this for I was a bit taken aback she suggested we pray together and we began to do so together.

At the end of this session she invited me to her home for lunch with her and her family. So, on the following Sunday I arrived at her home which was a large family house in Ewell village in Surrey. I entered feeling calm and happy. She made a special effort to make feel welcome and introduced to her family and her English husband. I offered to help with the preparation of the meal and we began to talk of this and many other things as we worked in her kitchen.

But I felt a little apprehensive. I was not sure why Mrs Wing was so friendly and felt a little wary. We met quite frequently for a while but after this when she suggested that it would be nice if I were to be baptised in the church I became unsure. She did persist in this for she was adamant that if I did not do so I would not be entitled to eternal life in heaven and this only served to unsettle me. This was certainly not what I had come to expect at all so I decided to stop meeting her and also stopped going to the church.

For a long time she continued to pursue me with visits, phone calls and little leaflets through the door but this became overwhelming and disturbed me even more. Suddenly, I felt that for me this side of my life was now over. I wanted to find my own way of believing, to discover what I felt was the truth and to do this I had to get away from Mrs Wing and her church and search for what I was looking for - but my way.

CHAPTER SIX
Seeing Beyond Reality

SHORTLY AFTER MAKING THE DECISION to find my own way to the truth about all things spiritual I stopped going to the Baptist church at Cheam in north Surrey. I carried on with the meditation because I found that quite relaxing and therapeutic whenever I could, which was most days then, I was able to withdraw from the great big busy world outside, sit in my room and connect to my inner world.

One day when I was at home and doing some dusting I was by the fireplace in the lounge when, and as I walked away, two of the candles in the holders shot out and fell to the floor. That did make me jump and, while I stood there for a moment or two collecting my thoughts, I realised that there had to be someone (or something) there with me. Even as these thoughts flew through my mind a wonderful feeling of peace and tranquillity came over me. I had never experienced such a thing before; it was so beautiful, as if I had no cares in the world. I could easily have welcomed such a feeling to have stayed with me.

Alas, this moment soon dissolved but the incident left me thinking that it was time I started to record and document these incidents and events. So, I decided to visit the local shop and get myself a decent size journal to keep a proper account of things.

Quite some time ago when I was much younger I had taken a four year training course to be a chef mostly because of my love of cooking It was about this time I was working for the Metropolitian Police Authority in their rather large station and complex in Sutton. I always enjoyed the work and had won several awards for my abilities, something that made me proud of my endeavours in this field.

But, I felt an urge to move on and thought I could better myself if I started my own catering business. It was all very well being ambitious in one direction but as I was growing in psychic stature and fully aware of my expanding abilities here I thought that I should take up something in which I might prove doubly useful to people.

I felt that I could not and would not limit myself any longer so the urge to leave the police work and start up on my own became so strong I set up a new business for myself: Occasions Caterers. Very early on in this new field of service to people I somehow knew that I was guided to a local Funeral Parlour where and with whom I had a long discussion. My thinking was on the line that newly bereaved folk simply wouldn't have the time to prepare food and drink for fellow mourners. So, I could step in a catering service for them.

This more than proved to be a good move and soon it became necessary to take on staff to help me. I remember making suitable thanks to my new friends in spirit for their advice and guidance. Sometimes I was so busy I had to hire staff to help me and the whole concept soon became what I called my bread and butter money,

But I was still interested in Spirit and developing my connection to the angels I carried on meditating and became very strict with my self-development. During my meditation sessions I would get very cold and still to the point where I could not feel my body and the next thing I was aware of was an eye in the middle of my forehead, staring at me. This was a strange affair but, curiously, not scary. I came to the conclusion this was my Guide looking after me by showing me the eye looking inward at me.

Books were immensely helpful at this point; I would read up as much as I could on the subject of the "third" eye and how it works. It was about now that I became aware that I was "seeing" images in my mind. One of the very first was of a telephone and then a coffin. I was afraid I was going to get a call about a death in the family, but shortly after the phone rang. Frederick Paine, the undertakers, wanted to know if I would contact a lady who had just lost her husband and needed someone to organise the catering. It was then it dawned on me that this was what I just had a vision about. So now I was being made aware of future events in my mind's eye. After the first time it didn't feel quite so scary in that when the phone did ring and I "saw" a coffin in my mind I knew it was more work coming in.

As time passed I began to have other equally strange experiences. Strange, that is to, for I was just getting used to my new acquired abilities and was never really sure of what was happening. One day I saw myself having a meal in a pizza restaurant and then about week later a friend and I ended up in such a place. Things were becoming more clear-cut with my new vision and my awareness of all the amazing things around me like just the leaves on trees, the vibrancy of all the colours made me feel as if a veil had been lifted for now I was seeing life from a totally different perspective - a more different reality.

Almost daily now the pictures, visions and similar experiences I was getting became stronger and stronger and events would unfold just as I was seeing them all in my mind. Then, one day I started seeing people who were no longer alive. My grandmother and grandfather were my first visitors.

Granddad would talk to me about his love of horses and racing and then he showed me the sweet shop in north London where he lived with Grandma. He even showed me my favourite sweets and how they were sold in those days. This connection with my family in spirit has always been a real comfort to me. I didn't need to try to get a message through to them for they just appeared and talked to me.

One event that has always made me aware of my abilities in those early days has always stood out in my mind. I remember that I had been hired to cater for a funeral when the family and the chief mourner, a widower, had left the house for the crematorium.

I started to prepare everything for their return when I realised that I could now see the deceased person in the lounge .Just briefly and in my peripheral vision the clocks went off and along with all the other noises, it was obvious that he was trying to get my attention.

This was something new and to say that I was a little scared at this point would have been putting it mildly, to say the least. However, I began to appreciate the irony of being watched by the man for whose mourners I was preparing the catering. I remember asking if he enjoyed my baking and he smiled back in approval. On another occasion a deceased woman told me that her husband had a thing about chocolate cake. I nodded appreciatively for he had made a point of asking me to make all of his guests a chocolate cake.

It soon became fairly clear as to why I was now successful at catering at funeral receptions for it was also quite obvious that I was there to help those left behind in such a way as to convey messages without it being too obvious that I was a medium – something that I would not mention to my clients. I was there to help out in more ways than one.

For around five years or so I spent much of my time catering at funeral receptions and rarely felt that I had not been of some extra assistance in some way for I was usually able to convey the right message without giving anything away.

But, I was becoming weary of the hard work involved and that, along with all the red tape began to take its toll on me as I started to lose the enjoyment (if that is the right word) and fulfilment that I found with such work. My third eye was now wide open and I could see that catering of this type was no longer to be a part of my personal future at all.

One day my large catering van was parked outside my house and I clairvoyantly saw a coffin in the back. This did perplex me somewhat but deep inside I realised that the time had come for me stop this kind of work.

I had no idea of what I was going to do next but, during a meditating session I felt drawn toward a Reiki course. Some time earlier I had been introduced to a lady called Dawn Hooper and after the initial interview and other preamble I signed up for the course which was held at Dawn's home in Catford, south London.

Dawn lived in a terraced house and when I first went inside it felt safe and warm and. The first day was spent becoming attuned to the healing symbols and learned about how the system worked. The first day over, I went home a tad light headed but ready for the next step. After finishing the first course and becoming reasonably proficient in the work I returned to Dawn for the Masters course to attune myself more fully. This was to prove to be a catalyst in my overall development for, after receiving this healing and new energy I now found it so profound it began to create a whole new change within me.

Images were now flooding into me thick and fast. So much so, that I had to speak to Dawn about it. Her advice was to try to close the third eye down and learn how to control it better that obviously was the time! Eventually I managed, to somehow become connected to my own angel and spirit friends for help. I felt confident that they could and would help and, sure enough they were very helpful. Despite all this I felt as though I was not slowing down so much but speeding up.

I knew I was open to spirit but I had to have an ordinary life as well because I was being taken over- used even. They seem so intent on using me as a vessel for their messages and healing it was becoming hard for me to too handle them properly. That I enjoyed the work was true, but there had to be some limits because I still had to live a normal life, if nothing else to help pay the bills!

In this interim period I got through several jobs but was fast becoming restless and that along with a feeling of no real direction I had to somehow stabilise all aspects of my life.

My guides now began to bombard me with requests to start readings for people using my gift of clairvoyance. They would help do whatever else might become necessary. I wasn't feeling too over-confident but their constant nudging was ever present. So, I began slowly asking people to come and see me. These early visitors I called my guinea pigs and I had plenty of volunteers of all ages to come along to my home and take part in a reading for free.

Again, in these early stages my messages were clear and from these small beginnings it all started to grow and then escalate. I just let it happen and made sure I stood well away from my ego and more or less surrendered to the spirits. This was an amazing thing to do because once they sense they have you they exude immense power far beyond the average comprehension. Of course, I also had to purge myself of any thought it was me doing the work.

After practising these readings I remember visiting my Mother's home shortly after I had completed the healing attuning course. She was complaining of a bad knee and I suggested that I tried to give some healing. We went in her conservatory overlooking her freshly mowed lawn - such a time when the grass always smells so fresh. I put my hands on her knee and we sat silently for a few minutes or so.

I could now see inside her knee when I saw a greyish mass area just by the tendons. It looked as if it were about to dissolve so I left my hands there. A short while later I gently let it go. She stood up and looked at me in amazement. She shook her leg, walked up and down and asked what I had done.

I told her that I had asked for help to heal and this was the result. We were both very surprised by what had happened and talked about the Reiki procedures. That my mother was a little sceptical was putting it mildly but a door was opening in her mind to the powers of healing.

My first Angel Workshop was at my house following on from some local advertising. Eight people turned up on the first night. The angels told me what to do and I followed their guidance. My mother had previously asked if she could sit in on the workshop and I let her. However, this proved to be a mistake. Many of the questions she asked put me on the spot in front of the others and I was quite upset with what I considered to be her upstaging me.

When it was over I asked why she had done that and although she said it was to help prepare me for possible problems I "knew" she wanted me to give this line of work up and pursue a more conventional path. That she was proud of me was obvious but she felt she couldn't brag about me in the same way as when I ran my own catering business. However, this was not to be my true calling – but working with the angels was.

This led me to me more careful for if my own mother was sceptical and obviously not rooting for me

then I had to be sufficiently wary as to who was so that I could more easily trust the people around me.

CHAPTER SEVEN

The Persistent Teenager

As my intuitive sight was so strong I decided to carry on with it, and I was giving more and more readings to clients this was the wish of my guides to do so, and people were coming from everywhere to see me and the more I used my gift the more clearer it became.

Rosemarie was busy with her teachings and I stopped seeing her because I was too busy myself but I never gave up on the Cards; I decided to use Angel cards as I preferred the images and gentleness of them the Tarot to me was rather harsh and I felt lower in vibration.

Things were ticking over nicely and I was working with an agency to bring in some extra cash to keep me afloat, my energy was drained by the work it was low paid and demoralising and I wanted to work for spirit full time so I attended as many fairs as I could to get out there and demonstrate my new found gift and help some people where ever I could.

My development was important to me as a healer and reader so I carried on with the meditation and sat quietly for at least 30 minutes a day to connect with the energy.

At around 4pm one Monday afternoon, I had the strangest experience! I felt the energy of a teenager around my body and my head especially; it was like he had taken over me completely, I saw my arms with tattoos and I was wearing a leisure suit and trainers which were scuffed up and un-done and generally unkempt in appearance.

My head had a big injury and I could see blood on the top of my crown the right side was injured Like it had taken a big blow.

"Who are you"? I said to this spirit, pausing for a while.......Sam he replied.

More and more of his energy enveloped me and he started showing me his habits like drug taking And drinking, I see him put a needle into his arm and I asked him to stop it and go away, but no He never did his persistent was irritating me so much, this was to be the strongest connection with spirit I had ever felt.

After begging with him to leave me I gave up, he started to show me a murder scene where he was murdered by two youths and his body being put in a car boot, he was so unrelenting to talk with me empathy was starting to creep in. He said he wanted me to find justice as he knew I worked for the police maybe you could find the killers he said.

No place was given to me, just the people and the car, and then the injury, this was shocking me so much- I never ever watched TV shows with this kind of graphic detail let alone have it around me so clearly projected from a young lad in spirit. Look I said! please leave me and step out of my Aura and go in peace to the light.

What on earth made him think I could help him I was no psychic detective either and this kind of stuff was not my forte, Sam decided to stay a while in fact he outstayed his welcome and around two weeks later, I got in touch with My friend Katrina whom was a police officer and told her all about Sam, in hope it would change things for him and that he could then find peace, as Justice was what he was looking for.

But alas Katrina had no records of such a missing teenager. So after this I called Rosemarie to help me with moving Sam on...

Unfortunately she was not too helpful and in fact rather uncooperative, reminding me that I had discontinued my work as a tarot reader and she was my mentor after all...

This is what happens when you mess around with spirit, she said;.

All I have been doing is meditating and reading books on the subject of Angels, She remained me of the importance of self protection when working spiritually, Rosemarie talked of spirit invasion and how they can take over you if you are not protected, well I had already experienced this at an earlier age when living alone. Maybe I had lots to learn still and this was to be another lesson!

I felt abandoned with Sam what next I thought, as he kept bouncing his ball around my bedroom

I am stuck with a teenager whom was murdered and he wants my help.

The hardest part for me was the feeling I had, a huge head injury, which I knew not to be true, but it felt so real as if it was mine.

I told my mother about Sam and she said it was Balderdash!, its true I said... within a flash she was calling all the psychics up whom lived locally to see if they could help, and with an angry tone said why does this keep happening to you. Her fear was her brother's anguish and untimely death regarding similar things washing over her like a dirty cloud.

I suppose I don't know enough to stop this if I can, I said in a calm voice, I called the spiritual church at Kingston and went for their advice as I trusted them implicitly. I was given a number of a lady called Heather a lady whom specialises in spirit release.

Heather and her partner were to come to my home and meet me and Sam!.

When they arrived I was so pleased to see them I invited them into my home and made some teas for us all and they sat on the edge of the sofa by the large window.

Heather had been doing spirit Release work for many years and was accompanied by her partner Thomas whom was also a light worker, he was not involved in the release process he was more of a chaperone and a driver for Heather.

After explaining all things that had been happening and Sam's attachment, Heather said he has not attached himself to you he has taken over you we call that possession, Well it certainly felt like that he was more than around me as it was so strong.

I had had so much of these spiritual visits I wanted it all to stop for good, I asked Heather to take it away, close me down do what you can to stop any more interference from the other side of life,

She could see my despair as I spoke.

She was very compassionate towards my plight and tried to explain that my gift was precious and I was to use it for good, then why all this negativity and spirit's coming to visit me all the time and upsetting me?, Heather said I would be mad to stop spirits helping me and how wonderful to have that in my life, I couldn't see that from where I was standing - You see I have ended up on a psychiatric ward in the past and it has not been much fun I can tell you.

She explained you have Angels around you and they look out for you and guide you protecting you always how lovely can that be!, Well I needed some serious convincing and we carried on with the Release.

The time was soon passing and we proceeded with the issue of Sam, First you need to call on your doorkeeper, this was to be a spirit guide whom watches over your crown chakra and only lets certain invited spirits in like a body guard in the spiritual realms. We settled down into a meditation and I invited my spirit guide in-at this time Sam was getting agitated and kept showing me how bored he was, I pushed him to one side and kept focused on my doorkeeper as I relaxed more and more I could see him more clearly he looked old and wore a robe he stepped forward and I had a few tingly sensations around my Aura at this point, I told Heather and she said he would always show some kind of sign for you to remember him by, I was glad because I felt I may have no more problems with lower entities and I was in control of whom came to me.

Then the crunch time came, Heather asked me to visualise a gate in the room and my door keeper standing guarding it, yes ok I said, then ask Sam to go towards the gate and walk through it to the Light so he can be free and happy in spirit, I asked Sam to do just that and I held his hand guided him forward and then passed his hand to my doorkeeper and comforted him, he walked through and went to the light.

I sigh of relief came over me "please let him be gone" I said out loud, I was not trusting enough of this and aired that to Heather and I then thanked my Aide for helping me.

I had to let go of my scepticism and trust and soon enough I would find out if Sam was still here or not.

After the session I offered a donation to Heather and we talked some more about her work and I mentioned that I was ready to see the positive side of spirit communication from now on and discover why I was here in the first place! Not in the physical sense but spiritually, what was spirit to do with me next-I knew I only wanted Angels around me and not anything lower in the future.

Heather and Tom left me with a business card should I need help again and advised me to go and sit in a circle and learn the skills of meduimship and development, I was not interested in this as I already had the gift of sight and contacting spirits I just wanted to to know how to control it that's all.

I felt everything was falling into place and I was meeting the right people at the right time life seemed to have meaning at last. I learnt how to protect myself psychically from a book called psychic protection and then practised it daily during my meditations and spiritual work, opening and closing down became very important to me as I wanted to avoid any more unwanted spirits popping in to say hello.

And with that I decided to sign up on a course in Angel development and awareness with Diana Cooper which was to take place in Kent at a spiritual retreat called the Seekers trust. I attended her course and qualified as an Angel teacher and was much wiser regarding spiritual things .

CHAPTER EIGHT
My Adhd Hell

SINCE I WAS LITTLE I have been quite a live wire, when I say that I mean I have had a drive and energy that was a bit erratic and scattered; I was not able to relax and was into this and that.

This was apparent to me when at school, as school was like a prison to me, I did not like the confines of that and this was maybe one of the reasons I spent a lot of time out of school rather than in it. As well as the bullying I endured, my spirit did not like restrictions and my resistance to go with the norm was strong, this was quite clear at an early age. I was labelled a dreamer, slacker and a bad student but although this hurt, the spirit is the spirit, you can't change that it is your divine make up.

I first started work at sixteen as a Dr's Receptionist; it was a local job near where we lived in Pimlico

This was followed by another job as a V.D.U operator in a merchant bank for a large company in London.

The first signs of ADHD were to be casting a shadow over me. Being in a office and sitting at a desk watching a clock was very difficult I was always finding a way to get away from my desk, I would visit the toilet many times during the day, or visit a friend on the floor below, I was to be reprimanded for this by the boss eventually.

I decided this job was not for me I was a creative soul who needed to express this to the world I started a course at a catering college shortly after and stayed there for 3 years I was in the flow of my creative self. The Nine to five thing was not me it sapped my energy.

Later in life I started to get many problems with employment not having work but staying in the work and seeing it through was the hardest part, I lacked self confidence due to being rejected as a child.

I was feeling embarrassed by my curriculum vitae, every time I went into a job as an employed person I felt a urge to leave soon after, things were going wrong and doors were closing. My overactive mind was running away with me, I just lived with it I was not aware of any problem just accepted this was me and got on with it.

The food business interested me a lot I loved to cook and bake from a child and won a cookery competion at the age of eight, I had many catering jobs until I went self employed which is what I loved the most, Freedom was my true desire and working for myself was amazing.

The truth be known I was not in alignment with my higher self and my sprit was restless and keen, but to do what I don't know at this point, ok I had an interest in spiritual things, but it was an interest, that's all.

People would comment on me being hyperactive and into this and that, I saw myself as a fun loving person whom loved to learn new things I went on so many course's I can tell you, But I didn't always finish things ! But also this was because I was free to choose what I learned and not be told what to learn there is a difference.

I had a thirst for knowledge in many things my mind was open and willing.

It was in my mid forties that the penny was to drop after so many jobs and seeing my impulsive behaviour I cried out loud to myself what is wrong with me, I knew something wasn't right I asked my angels for help please tell me why I am so restless and can't hold a job down please I begged them.

Shortly after I was shown the word ADHD, it kept coming to me, so I looked on line and read the symptoms and I felt completely numb I was reading about how I was!, and I had been for so long.

In fact I felt I had this since I was little but no one did anything or guided me to see anyone Maybe it was not heard of when I was a child, but apparently if you had the symptoms as a child then you will also as an Adult.

The type of symptoms a Child with ADHD would have are:-
Poor Organisational skills
Trouble starting and finishing projects
Constantly losing or misplacing things
Lack of confidence
Frequently Interrupt others or talk over them (this was

my problem, mum would always say let me finish what I
am saying)
Figgiity
Act spontaneously without regard or Consequences
Can't sit still
Loss interest quickly
Lack of focus
And on and on.......

I remember a day when I was making bunting in the kitchen
with my in-law for a summer fete, I walked away and started
gardening and left her to it "what are you doing she said", I just got
distracted and went onto something else, completely unaware of
it-this was typical of ADHD syndrome.

The thing is a women can multi-task but can you begin to
imagine a women mutli-tasking who had ADHD... well it was
quite funny I was doing five jobs at once sometimes, You feel highly
energetic and perpetually on the go as if driven by a motor this was
because a part of the brain was running to fast!. The best metaphor
I can give is imagine a car engine and the rev counter was stuck,
well something along those lines, this was the Hyperactivity side
of the problem exhaustion got the better of me eventually.

When I told my husband about the problem, I just broke down
again and into his arms, He said he did notice my behaviour and
just accepted it as me, but also he did see how negative it was
and highlighted the issues that were affecting me the most, but
completely with love and compassion he supported me.

The Dore foundation was an organisation whom helped people whom suffer with such tendencies, they had an on- line quiz to test your severity, I did the quiz and I got a high score...

I broke down crying again really seeing why I had had problems in my life with concentration etc.

A cloud had been lifted at last.

The next thing I did was to ring the organisation up and tell them of my findings.

The lady was very empathetic she advised me to see my GP," I am not taking drugs I said," She said Your high score is affecting your life my advice is to see your dr as soon as you can and see what they can do to calm your mind- The good news was that it was controllably and the Dore foundation helped me find a solution. But eventually I turned to Holistic approaches i.e. Meditation, changing my diet, and taking lots of Omegas to help.

The results were amazing. I was in control at last.

ADHD was discovered in 1902 and was shown to be a biological factor affecting the brain especially the frontal lobe which is the part associated with impulse control and reasoning, tests showed the frontal lobe was smaller in children with ADHD, also the neurotransmitter dopamine was lower This is why motivation, mood attention and learning was affected.

Hundreds of children today are being labelled as destructive and hyperactive, but thank god it has at last been discovered that it is biological and not just behavioural. It can be treated with drugs should a parent choose that route.

But one thing that I discovered was that some of the world's greatest entrepreneur such as Richard Branson,Opray winfrey, and Steve Jobs founder of Apple all have ADHD and they have tapped into the positive side of the condition, such as:-

Lateral thinking
Intuition
Sponsenatity
Creativity
Fearlessness
Impulsivity
And used this to their advantage.

These things would make most people wince!, You see having ADHD makes you feel alive, it makes you want to think outside of the box and I can tell you many a time I have stepped outside my comfort zone, and because of that I have made good things happen.

The special conditions that unlock the genius behind ADHD are not encouraged or even taught In society.

Most people with adhd would feel suppressed if they don't tap into the traits that it brings.

My usual approach would be to ask the universe for help as well, this is when I discovered the Archangel Metatron, he is the Angel of Motivation and helps children with ADHD focus and concentration.

After meditating on Him I was soon starting to get amazing help I was very focused and my paper work especially was put in order.

Today I believe that mostly I have been taken away from the path I choose for myself and have been guided onto a spiritual one by Angels, why I ask myself have such phenomenal things happened to me the philanthropy of this work was very fulfilling more so than catering.

CHAPTER NINE
The Marriage Warning

THE ANGELS WERE HELPING ME with so many things I was guided to what I asked for and all the signs like feathers and coins etc were everywhere to see, I was also seeing Angels clairvoyantly and my own Angel Amber was around me a lot.

I had always wanted to connect with the ocean and felt drawn to learn scuba diving I joined a local club in Kingston upon Thames and was excited about learning the skills involved and having my first Dolphin encounter I have always wanted to connect with Dolphins.

The club always booked weekends away in the UK and abroad I started using my new skills around the Northumberland coast in a place a called The Farne Islands which was well known for its flocks of birds especially Puffins whom nest their every year and was well known for sea lions as well

The day was going well and we all went out on the boat to Dive and I was about to enter the water with my instructor Harold but inside I was afraid, feathers were floating on the surface near the boat; my solar plexus was jumping around So I felt a little trepidation as to whether to enter the water!.

I knew my instructor would take care of me and we both signalled to each other the OK sign which is sign language for lets enter the water, we leapt forward and found ourselves on the surface of the cold water bobbing about I was still feeling agitated, but again just went with it.

Harold pointed his thumb down and we descended into the waves.

Shortly after landing on the ocean bed we adjusted ourselves then Harold was having difficulties with his equipment and bubbles were escaping from his regulator at a rapid speed I could hardly see him for Bubbles were all over the place he looked me in the eye and before I knew it he was ascending to the surface, holding onto me and pulling me upwards! this is a very dangerous thing to do in Diving you must always ascend slowly or you could end up with a Bend! (A term used for nitrogen overload)

As a novice I was in his hands and literally being dragged to the surface like an uncontrolled rocket.

Upon surfacing Harold removed his mask and waved to the boat to rescue us.

I said what happened as I gasped for breath, Harold was a little embarrassed and saved his breath until we was safe on board the boat.

The crew wanted to know why we surfaced and Harold went onto explain his regulator was faulty and he apologised for scaring me but he had no choice but to take me with him as I was his student he could hardly leave me sitting at the bottom of the sea alone.

What was apparent was the fact that the Angels gave me all the signs and warnings before hand the feathers floating near the boat and the solar plexus jumping around and getting warnings there.

So why didn't I listen to the signs, maybe I was to learn from this that the Angels don't mess when they want you to take notice of a serious situation listen to that inner voice. I had a lot to learn in trusting my Intuition.

The other trips were all very pleasant and I learned to dive and got my Badge, I then went off to fulfil my dolphin dream in Bali.

The next dive trip was to be the Queens Golden Jubilee weekend and it was to be a special one for me I was to meet my future husband who also was a Diver he was more advanced than me, Simon was a kind guy I felt a good energy from him.

Plymouth was a regular place the club went to and the festivities were well and truly under way to remember the Queens jubilee the day was idyllic the beautiful sun out on the boat and the evening sitting on a hilltop looking over the crowds enjoying the live music and fireworks display.

The next thing I knew was my heart was filled with the most astounding feeling of Love all encompassing Love like my Heart Chakra had burst open and A hundred Angels were dancing around inside of me, euphoria, lightness and delight are a few words to describe it, I can't put the feeling into words as I looked over at Simon I knew it was not love for him but just Love in its most vibrant form inside me I was so happy and alive at that moment I will never forget it. I felt the Angels were around me this evening.

After about two weeks Simon and I started dating, He was a shy person but easily led by the others in the dive group those that were into drugs and drinking and skylarking would include Simon like they always had before I came along, This did put doubts into my mind, but we carried on seeing each other and I hoped he would not be so easily led in the future.

I have never been a drinker and preferred a cup of tea mostly as my tipple, Simon would take me out for meals and sometimes he would drink and drive which also upset me as we was 8 years apart maybe he was not so mature as me, I kept dismissing the negative stuff, and just saw the divine in him.

I was still doing my course at the Diana Cooper school at this time, I started to get voices in my head saying "stay single" this would not go away, I asked my group why this was as I was In love with Simon and I did not want to stay single I had been single for 10 years and was ready for another relationship , admittedly in hind sight I was not seeing what was apparent and choose to ignore it

They say love is blind.

They asked me to take an Angel card the card was the ANGEL OF DISCERNMENT well I was truly being asked to discern whom was telling me to stay single was it an Angel or another spirit or was the card about Simon discerning if he was right for me or not Confusion took over me and I carried on seeing Simon whilst a whisper in my head would not go away telling me to stay single.

I was getting visions of a Diamond ring and then he proposed to me after a year of courting.

I said yes despite my inner voice telling me not to.

We married in Turkey near the beach with 36 guests it was a beautiful ceremony, When we got back home to the UK I sold my 3 bed detached house and invested the money into a new Home in Kent, in fact I felt drawn to live near the seekers trust and other Spiritual retreat places around that area.

After 2 years of marriage the differences were beginning to surface more strongly I was very spiritual and like to live a peaceful life filled with inspiration and joy, Simon family were more 9-5 people whom believed the only way to make money and live was through struggle and discipline and not creatively joyfully, especially my mother in law she saw me creating a dream job and kept saying it won't work get a normal job... Knuckle down and be miserable like the rest of us, no one can make a living from a dream she was trying to make me see her reality, I felt alienated I had to listen to this constantly and dreaded her visits to my home she would comment on my spiritual statues around the house of Buddha etc and I was so far apart from their world it was painful.

Simon would carry on drinking and was often trying to get me to join him, His mother introduced him to drink at the age of 12 she said it was good to let a child see drink as not a bad thing as long as it was done in moderation, Well after having to pick him up from London when he knocked himself unconscious and was covered in blood with a head injury was hardly my idea of sensible drinking,

I had to take him to casualty to many times, the drunken abuse was coming at me thick and fast and my heart was sinking as the true person was revealed to me.

As I grew more and more spiritually and worked more with light and helping people with my healing
   I found myself living with a person whom was into darker things the two worlds collided like asteroids clashing as they met. I was not the same person I was before and I could not relate to any of my friends I had known for years either, slowly people were drifting out of my life. The spiritual path was starting to be a lonely one.

I was told to remove my spiritual Images and statues, each time we got a visit from his family as they did not understand such matters, I went along with this to keep the peace, it was like I was suppressing myself hiding my spirituality behind a veil to protect them from what !?......

Life was getting more and more down as the time went by. When Simon was sober he was a nice person helpful kind and loving, he often would follow me to work and I was feeling so hemmed in
   I needed to escape his possessive nature, although he did not like my interest in spiritual things he maybe could have benefited from the peace and contentment that permeated my being and the protection I had around me.
   I went off for a weekend on a cookery course and to have some time to self....
   I felt a inner urge to leave the course a few hours early and head home a couple of hours along the motorway and I was back in Kent, as I entered my home I was strongly guided to turn on the computer, Simon was in the garden at the time.

As I did I pressed search history no Idea why! I just did, I was then to see the most shocking images before me of what Simon was looking at prior to myself getting home, My heart sank How could he!!

I was guided by the angels to see my husband's darker side, it was a wakeup call.

I confronted him and I threw my wedding ring on the table and left the house in a hurry.

I cried inconsolably at the truth and it was all making sense to me now. The man I married was into drink and other dark dark things that was not what I wanted for myself I wanted a person whom embraced the light.

So all the warnings were from the Angels and again I had not listened to this, maybe I had to learn how to notice a warning sign and how it comes to you in many forms.

I stayed away from Simon for a few days and when I went home I tried to forgive him as he was happy with the way he was, my higher self wanted me to forgive, but this overshadowed my relationship and rather than end the marriage I carried on so as not to upset Him and live a lie for five more years.

Then after many card messages to leave and move on I finally decided it was for both of our sakes that we parted so he could find a person more liking to himself and I also.

With the news Simon was to rip down all my Angel pictures and trinkets were cut away from inside my car I felt my heart had been trampled on as if a part of me was being hurt personally.

He knew that my world revolved around Angels and Healing so that's how he hurt me back.

So after nine years of Marriage I felt it was another lesson in listening to the whispers so to speak, this lesson was to cost me dearly as I lost my home during the divorce and were to be homeless as a result, I approached the housing association in a bid to get some where to live and 6 month later I was offered a flat in a nice new built development.

I had to sign for this and take on the tenancy in quite a hurry I had no time to think, although I really wanted a house.

So after getting the keys to the property we went about Decorating it my family helped out and I could see a light at the end of all this.

Then I started to see a coffin in the Lounge of the flat, Oh no what now I thought to myself, not more problems, I was also due to meet my brother on a Saturday morning to decorate the lounge we agreed to meet at 8am, well I could not find the keys to let us in I looked frantically everywhere, but no Keys.

Ok I thought no keys to get in and a coffin in the lounge were these signs from the universe to not move in; I could not turn a blind eye this time!!... I was more aware than ever before of universal messages.

I decided to cancel the tenancy agreement and forgo the new home and stay put in my marital home

I knew the universe had better plans for me somewhere down the line and I really did want a new house with a garden so I looked at this as a blessing in disguise.

So again I found myself as a Single person I had a deep feeling that my soul was here to do bigger things and I had to be free to follow that guidance I was ready to embrace my intuition and follow that calling, I felt more connected to my Angels I was having wonderful dreams of Rainbows and Coins which were to restore my faith in Angelic guidance as I felt so supported.

I was getting so many people coming to me and seeing results of the Healing and Guidance I was giving it felt very natural and easy, the words just flowed from my lips as if a higher presence was talking through me.

I kept my ego in check and reminded my clients that it was not me doing the work but my higher self

Was helping me to help them.

My manifestation was also working a treat as I worked on Affirmations and Visualisation to help with everything I was seeing the amount of power available to us all to transform our very existence

I passed this knowledge on to people and helped empower them.

CHAPTER TEN

Saved By A Carnival Angel

It was a cold January day and I was at home heavily involved in my regular domestic usual chores wondering how this New Year was going to pan out for me. At such a quiet time one of the best methods is to consult your own personal pack of Tarot cards.

So, I found my own pack, sat myself down on a couple of comfortable cushions on my nice blue bedroom carpet, shuffled the cards and mentally asked the Angels to help me look ahead. I laid the cards out in a spread for a one year forecast.

For those who don't know how to do this one of the best ways is to simply lay them out in such a way that each calendar month is represented by a single card. You can achieve this by creating a "clock face" design and, when you place a card in the middle it represents you. When I had finished laying the spread I became a little uneasy as the cards for the months of August and September were The Devil and the Tower respectively.

This made me think for some time and I can honestly say that it didn't do my nerves any good the more I did try to fathom it all out. Just what was ahead for me, I wondered, and in particular, what was in store for August and September? Eventually, I picked up the cards, slipped them back in the pack and put them away thinking that whatever might be going to happen was going to occur anyway – there was little I could do about it. .

Spring came and went, summertime approached and by the time we were in the middle of it all I had more or less forgotten the spread of the cards and their possible portent. I got in touch with a very good friend of mine, Lucy a friend who had just returned from her holiday and we decided to get together and visit the London Carnival. This was a useful idea because she lived in a small flat right in the middle of where it all takes place.

I caught an early morning train to travel up to London on the first day of the Carnival and by the time I reached central London I began to feel a tad uneasy again. I became anxious and concerned and, for some reason, was just not myself. By the time I arrived at her station a feeling of heaviness hung around me along with a sense of foreboding that I could not explain.

In the street outside the station the police were placing crowd barriers everywhere to keep the area safe but the atmosphere felt very heavy to me, There were only a very few people about that early and the closer I got to her flat the more I felt that there was what I can only call a strange presence in the air.

Lucy was expecting me and, once she had made us a much needed coffee, we caught up on her holiday gossip and other matters. During the course of the morning more friends arrived and the general excitement of the impending Carnival day took centre stage between us, Actually, that was not strictly true for I still felt that there was something not quite right – but I didn't let on to the others because I didn't want to spoil their day over something about which I was still unsure.

The sounds outside began to increase and we could hear the music starting up, the drums with their rhythmic beat throbbing and almost calling everyone to come and enjoy themselves. I popped my head out of the window and saw some of the dancers in their colourful costumes parading down the street with some of the visitors dancing along with them...We all agreed it was time to get outside ourselves and join in the fun so off we went to join in the throng.

By now I just wasn't feeling myself at all. I felt awful and full of trepidation. The sight of a collection of people wearing hooded tops didn't really help either. I then started worrying about what those tops might be hiding. It simply wasn't now my cup of tea at all.

After five or so minutes of this a feeling of fear came over me and there was a strange heavy pressure on my right arm like something pressing down on it all the time. I tried to brush it off but, of course, I couldn't see it although I could certainly feel it. Then the sensation of whiteness became clearer in my mind's eye. I thought this was strange as I kept trying to brush the feeling away. I also half wondered what other folk might be thinking as they thronged past.

Because of these different experiences I made my apologies to my friends by suggesting that I had an upset stomach and would feel better if I went back to Lucy's flat. I implied that I would see them all later on and that they were to carry on and enjoy their day.

As I made my way slowly back to the flat I could still feel the energy of the pressure on my arm but, once I got inside the flat

I felt a little easier in myself. I went over to the window to look outside when all those feeling became more intense. I became more anxious and then I found myself frantically trying to open the window with the intention of jumping out.

At this point I was pulled back by something in the room tugging on my left arm and I found myself running away from the window. I flew into the bedroom and almost fell on to my friend's bed, shaking like a leaf.

Suddenly, on the wall opposite her bed the words "Saved by the Angels" appeared. I just couldn't understand any of this at all. I had no idea of what was happening to me - only that it was!

Somehow or another, I began to calm down a bit so I made my way to her kitchen and made myself a cup of camomile tea. While I sat there clutching this soothing drink I once again try to understand what was going on and began to mull it all over and over all over again.

A short while later my friends returned and I explained that as I wasn't feeling too well I was going to go home. I said nothing about what I (thought I) had experienced for I was sure they might not understand or ask too many questions that I couldn't answer.

The journey home was fairly uneventful and, on returning home headed for the safety of my own bedroom. I wrote down everything that had happened and started to appreciate that I had an Angel Intervention of some kind.

The following morning I went to my local Spiritualist church in order to thank the Angels for their life saving act. As I sat down at the front of the church on the empty chair between another lady and me there was a book that lay in such a way I could clearly read the title: "Saved by the Angels" by a Glennyce Eckersley.

Now, not only was this a vindication of what I had been through it was also a rather simple but unerringly accurate summing up of the whole affair. I became drawn to the woman next to me and asked her if the book were hers she agreed that it was and I felt myself telling the whole story of what I had been through. I also asked if I might buy the book and she agreed

Upon leaving the church I was at peace with myself, a shade light-headed perhaps but, somehow "knowing" that my faith was much renewed in Guardian Angels.

Later on, I telephoned Lucy to offer my apologies and an explanation for my quick absence, she was fine with it although I kept it to myself.

After I then rang Katrina a Police officer friend of mine who had been working on duty at the Carnival, a chill ran down my spine when she said that she was on duty that day and went on to tell me one of the more gruesome events of the day was when she had to attend to the aftermath of a woman who had jumped from a window and killed herself!. My jaw dropped and a chill ran down my spine oh my god that could have been me.

In the circumstances I thought that now might be a good time to explain what had really happened to me. Knowing me and my interests rather well she expressed her amazement at what I said

I had been through. We both were amazed at the events that unfolded that day and later met to have a talk over a nice latte.

Since then, I have had several experiences of a similar nature. One or two were not too good but the others were quite pleasant. However, all have served to remind me that that we do all have our own Guardian Angel on our shoulder.

I called in the Angels to my home and
then this white light appeared

The Light started to move around and change
shape it stayed for ever after that.

During the evening I would turn the lights out to see the energy without a flash on my camera it showed as a white circle mostly it can bee seen with the naked eye very well

During the day it would just stay close to me
when I was talking to clients on the phone
It rarely moved from my side.

After sending someone some distant healing they
told me this wing had appeared on their kitchen
window and also some white light in background if
you look closer you can see it, it was my most
Precious confirmation of the Angels working with me.

Archangel Michael showed his sword of
Protection over my house many times

After my home move and trepidation about it all going well , this rainbow greeted me the first day it showed up on the carpet.

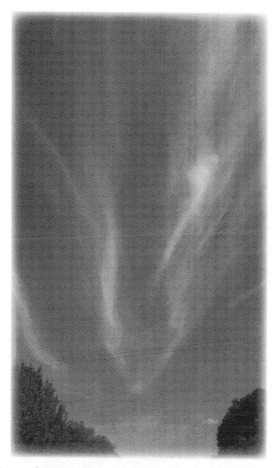

I was driving along a main road near home and I
saw this huge pair of cloud shaped wings,
I wanted to take a picture so I pulled over and took these photos
And I heard a voice after say TURN IT UPSIDE DOWN!.
There I saw Mother Mary holding Jesus
in her arms I was amazed.

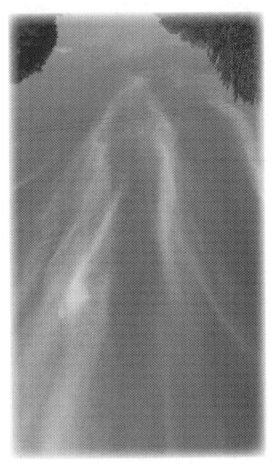

If you look at the picture upside down you will see her
She has always told me I have work with children to do.

PART TWO

On The Path At Last

CHAPTER ELEVEN

The Angels On The Plane

WHEN I WAS SEVENTEEN MY best friend of the time and I flew to Jersey for a holiday. I recall that we flew with British Airways on a flight that barely lasted forty-five minutes in the air. Nevertheless, the flight was so bumpy at one stage I thought my number was up. I remember holding on tight with little or no idea as to whether we would make it or not. The experience put me off flying anywhere again – well, for a while, anyway!

A little later on I had a few hypnotherapy lessons and bought a CD to help me with this problem. It helped in as much that I knew that if I had that sort of trouble again my flying days were over. I did fly again – but not a little thing with propellers but on a big comfy jet. Once my connection with angels had grown stronger I booked trips without thinking twice about what was involved. I chose to leave my worries until nearer the time but it was mostly wasted energy as a rule.

I remember that I had to book a flight to Bali, perhaps the longest flight I had ever taken - eighteen hours nonstop. How was I going to manage that I wondered? Some two weeks before the flight I was shown a cross on the tail of the plane that I took that as a sign of protection. I know that I prayed for the Archangel

Raphael to be there but it was the Archangel Michael who was to be with me for he appeared before me in all his glory.

Even before I arrived at the airport I had another vision of my luggage on the conveyor belt going around and around with me standing their waiting to collect it. The more fear I experienced the more visions I was getting from the angels. Then I saw my luggage safe and sound at the hotel reception desk. Obviously this was amazing and comforting, but still not quite enough to make me relax so just how much more reassurance did I need?

Just prior to boarding the plane I "saw" feathers on the engines while the cockpit was shown to me, all the dials had large ticks on them as if to say all was in working order. On this journey as I sat in my seat I saw several cherubim on the nose with polish in one hand and dusters in other polishing the nose making it all nice and shiny. I know I laughed out loud at this for I felt this showed a great sense of humour in their attempts to relax me.

As we taxied along the runway the Archangel Michael appeared to me rather larger than life under the aircraft. His wings were so big they looked larger than the plane itself. I felt quite in awe of him for he was wearing a blue cloak with his sword tucked into a belt around his robe. He was there to help the plane and protect the travellers on this particular Bali trip. For him to have appeared like this was amazing and I silently thanked him for such protection. Now I really felt honoured for once we were airborne he came with us to help us high into the skies. I was so overcome at this sighting that my eyes welled up as the fear dropped away and I felt completely safe.

The trip was smooth and during the flight I had many visions of my holiday in Bali. It was so exciting to be able to travel to these wonderful places. When we approached the airport for Bali prior to landing the Archangel Michael again appeared to me as if to show me the plane would make a safe landing.

On many future journeys it seemed that Michael almost never left me when I needed him the most. I recall that one journey was not that smooth but I began to receive messages that all was fine and that there was no need to worry. The words "You are OK" came to me in my head and on the head rest in front of me the words "You are Safe" appeared. .So, if was I was scared at any time these messages were obviously meant to be reassuring that I knew I could relax.

In 2007 I was due to fly out to Ibiza for a week for a course and on arrival at Stansted Airport I felt fine. I was receiving my usual signs and visions from the angels about the trip but even as I was aware of these messages I also kept seeing a message warning me to not board the plane. This made me most apprehensive indeed. I asked my guides about all the positive signs I was receiving yet this warning message now seemed to be appearing everywhere. It was really quite confusing.

I did not discuss this with the other students with whom I was travelling for I had no physical or any tangible evidence and I didn't want to alarm anyone. I remember finding some where quiet to sit so that I might be alone. Here I could be apprehensive without the others being aware. Suddenly, a message came through on the loud speaker system from the flight operator that a technical fault had been discovered on the plane and that we were to take another plane.

Now I realised what the warning was all about. The engineers obviously knew their stuff and while checking things out they had found the problem, thankfully before we took off. It didn't really matter that much to me though because I would never had boarded the plane even though all seemed fine at the time. As it happened all was not OK and the angels knew exactly why which is why when I do travel any great distance I tend to tune into the Archangel Michael for his blessings. If he says things are fine, then I travel truly grateful for his love and protection.

CHAPTER TWELVE

Seeing My Mother's Death

IN JUNE 2008 I WAS going about my usual daily routine when I suddenly "saw" a Coffin in my mother's bungalow. Almost immediately I heard warning bells began to sound and it was rather alarming. As far as I was aware mum was well and fit as a fiddle. Then I thought that perhaps she was thinking of moving house. You see, to me a coffin symbolises endings – and that could be anything like, for example, a place, a job, or a home.

However, this image was now appearing to me quite frequently so I tried to tell my sister Suzy of this without raising any unnecessary alarms. And when I enquired if she knew that mum might be planning to move she said she had no idea either way.

With this in mind I managed to carry on but did ask of my guides for their help for I was greatly concerned and just could not shift my feeling of dread. My mother had been living in her place for about two years so I could see no reason for a move on her part. When I put my rather sceptical brother in the picture in respect of my feelings he showed little or no interest at all. So my sister and I kept our own counsel and made no effort to find out if our mother did, in fact, have any moving plans because we both knew she loved her little home.

As the months went by I still felt that my mother might be forced to move home or have a problem of that kind. As the autumn approached and when I was visiting her she began to tell me of her blood pressure problems and how she had to monitor the problem on a day to day basis. If it were too high then she would have to have something prescribed by her doctor to reduce it.

I often have premonition dreams and in the following early March I was dreaming about praying to a god, when the process seemed to be interrupted by my becoming aware of a room filled with mattresses with people sleeping on the floor and then I saw a churchyard full of headstones.

I woke up and made a note of the dream. I felt nothing in respect of my mother but then I saw the coffin again this time much more clearly - and it was in her lounge. My immediate reaction was to send her a text on my mobile phone but as I could get no reply I followed this up with a call but her phone was engaged.

Then later on that afternoon my brother telephoned and told me that my mother had died from a heart attack. I scarcely heard much more of what he said for I was just so inconsolable but he arrived a little later on and when we got to mum's place much of the rest of the family were there. It is never really pleasant at such times for anyone irrespective of the relationship they may have had with those who have passed on and the grieving period is almost always hard for those of us left behind.

The dream was now a reality the praying to god and matresses on the floor was true as we all had to sleep at my sisters home on make shift beds!. On arrival at my mother's home I heard that my sister was in the room where my mother lay talking to her as though she was still with us physically. My brother and I also went in and, together - but alone so to speak, we spent some time with our thoughts of our dearly departed mother.

Despite everything, this was a total shock but I had seen it coming. I was upset that I never wanted to see the truth and was in denial so I asked the Angels why show me my mother's death. But I did not accept that the last thing I was going to see was that she was going to pass over.

In the weeks that followed I became aware that my mother was never really very far away and she would often speak to me calling me by a very private nickname she had always had for me. This helped ease the pain a lot and, as time moved on so the healing process began to take shape.

But the hardest moments were to come on the day of her funeral it was hard to endure but even then she was never far away. On the days leading up to the funeral where there was much activity to organise I got through it all quite unperturbed and swiftly making special arrangements that would of made her smile from heaven. I knew she wanted us all to be at peace about her leaving us.

The funeral took place in Sutton it amazed me to see how much she had been loved for so many people were there to say their last goodbyes. After the funeral I was sent some of the photographs of the horse drawn carriage and when I looked through them I could see that her Glass carriage had been covered in rainbows the colours were all over her coffin I knew then that she was one of the "Light" workers and that the angels had been there to help us through the day. This was a lovely moment for me and I felt very calm and peaceful.

After you lose someone life certainly changes. You become much more aware of your own mortality almost as a wakeup call to follow your heart and live life to the full. I had such an experience and was now ready more than ever to work with spirit.

Some twelve months or so later when I was not really feeling quite my usual self and not as motivated as I could have been I heard a bird noise in the house. I did not know where it was coming from although I could hear the chirping quite clearly but when I woke the next morning and went into the kitchen I found a small sparrow on the floor. It was lame and hardly moving. This little thing had also lost its mother.

I felt quite helpless as I picked the little thing up and began to ask for healing for it. In the garden I found a little place to for it to rest it was a hanging basket that was empty but for soft soil I knew he would be safe there and start to get better, but for as long as I held the poor little mite it snuggled up taking the warmth from my hands and, presumably, felt safe.

I felt that this was a message and that I now understood what was required of me. I had suffered a loss and was feeling lost but I had learned few lessons and gained an experience that I was able to translate when needed into being a comfort and support for others at their time of loss.

I needed to get back on track and heal myself.

CHAPTER THIRTEEN

Trusting Spirit

*"Intuition is a spiritual faculty that does not
explain but simply points the way."*
(Florence Scovel Shinn - Spiritual Writer.)

THIS IS AN INTERESTING TOPIC for even though you see that we all
have free will, we let our ego get in the way rather than listen to the
inner voice override it. This often leads to chaos, disorganisation
and disappointment.

For example, how many times have you had an idea but left
it and done your own thing only to find that had you pursued
the scheme it would have been the best decision if only you had
followed it through?

I have learned the hard way and I am afraid too many choices
in my life have been made without sufficient thought. Thus, I have
often found that what I did do was not such a wise choice after
all. Having "ADHD" has not exactly been much of a help either
for this makes one very impetuous – almost as if reasoning does
not exist. Our higher selves are wise and much more able to know
"us" than our "ego" selves so my advice would be to trust the spirit
when making decisions.

I will give you an example to explain this. One day I was looking for some crystals and was searching the Internet and seemed to be "Googling" everything I could. Some companies didn't respond while others did. Certain crystals were far too expensive and so I gave up. Then I asked my higher self to help find the crystals I needed for I was in something of hurry in that I was about to conduct a workshop.

I was directed to a small shop in my own village of West Malling that sold ornaments and candles and so on and found exactly what I was looking for and all at a very reasonable price but unfortunately there was none in stock. The owner was very helpful and offered to get some for me from her wholesaler and get back to me the following day. However, then I would be on my way to the Greenwich market to do some shopping with my daughter so I suggested that while I was still looking and that time was an issue, she could go ahead but that if saw what I wanted I would buy them then and there. She was very helpful and agreed to this arrangement.

When my daughter and I arrived at the market local people told me of a crystal shop nearby so off I went. This time this shop had not only the right crystals at much better prices but I also found a necklace which had an angel with an amber stone attached to it. So I got more than I expected and was very happy.

This was a good demonstration of surrendering to your higher self for when reasonably developed it will take care of a lot of hard work for you. The spirit may tends to have better choices or plans that you cannot always be aware of but it is dislikes resistance because this blocks the flow of your energies.

In another example to illustrate these points was when I had been invited to attend an "holistic fayre" in a Buckinghamshire village one lovely summer day in a July. I felt that this would be a good idea so I promptly booked a stall, hired some help and never really thought about it again.

However, on my journey I noticed a few spiritual signs which are not like the road signs you see when out travelling although I still had to make diversions on the journey anyway but after much delay and frustration I finally arrived,

What a waste? The event was one terrible failure in that so few turned up and my return journey was almost as full of problems as the outward one had been. Perhaps if I had got in touch with my higher self and thought some more I may well have saved a wasted day along with all the disappointment.

It costs nothing to tune into the higher self and ask for guidance but how many of us actually do this is another story. For me this was a learning curve and, until one has these experiences, one can't have more positive affairs because these were good lessons in trusting the spirit to take care of me and heaven only knows I have had many.

I began to get visions of me writing books where I would dream about typewriters. At first I brushed these away as fantasy. I asked myself how I might write a book but in spite of my doubts I began to receive more and more visions as well as having spiritual messages of me composing such a work. I must admit, my original views of authors were as an elite few most of whom were in a vastly different league to me.

On the other hand, I had always loved reading since I was a child and still do, but writing one? Well with my condition (ADHD) it would be a miracle to sit still for five minutes but an inward burning desire would not let me dismiss the idea. It was when I asked the spirit to find me some help I came across three authors and an editor almost within two weeks – and that was when I began to question if my path might be about writing.

Then, one day while idly toying with my angel cards I found several of them mentioning that I might write. One of the card was Thoth, the Egyptian Sun God of writing and another was Metatron who is known to help children with ADHD problems and who is the keeper of the Akashic Records. So, after getting all of this rather positive feedback from my spiritual friends I removed my blocks and began to plan.

For me self-help books have always been a source of growth and learning so I was drawn to this subject quite strongly. After all, I was helping people one to one now but felt that I should now move on to help people with my words. I remembered how much resistance I came up against with my own demons. At about this time I also began to notice several mediums and clairvoyants telling me I was going to write and they told me so quite definitely. I felt that my life and paranormal experiences were now to be aired to demonstrate to others how much help is at their finger tips so to speak for writing is not an easy task.

After all the experiences I have had have obviously not been in vain I believe that my dilemmas have more than helped me to help others who were having the same events and happenings as I used to have.

Thus, I am now more than able to show them the way.

PART THREE

A Guide To Psychic Communication And Protection

CHAPTER FOURTEEN
Raising Your Vibration

FOR ME THE CHANGE HAPPENED a long time ago now. It was shortly after I had taken the Reiki attunement course. I remembered being drawn to this system as a way of becoming closer to the angels.

I have always thought that I have been attracted to positive energy generally and when I was young I did not drink and smoke like my friends. It just didn't suit me possibly because I felt very different from the others in my circle. Now, of course, it all make sense for was born into this world as a worker in the light so, quite naturally, I would not become engaged in such activities.

As we move into the Age of Aquarius we are aware of the many changes in the world for this is where we will be able to step up to claim our true power as spiritual beings and creators of our own lives. Many people are already beginning to experience the move upward from the more lowly activities to the rather more attractive higher and spiritual events of life. The herd mentality is fast slipping away from people where it has dominated our consciousness for so long.

I see clients all the time who feel life must have more to offer than their present way of life. They want to explore all these new possibilities to help "find" their inner selves and bring out the passion that helps them to feel alive and creative. But first much must change, not on the outside but on the inside where the soul is crying out for more expression, more freedom, truth and the real connection to the source of our energies.

As one expands and shift we will intuitively know what is right or is not for us. This can often seem to be very painful to face for these changes apart from meaning growth also means that we have to become far more self-aware than ever. So, when you ask for help to improve your way of life you have to be prepared to work hard and become much more positive to make it all happen. Changes like this must first occur within then the physical changes will be easier to manage and maintain outwardly.

To connect more properly with the angelic realms to gain the assistance you seek you will need to need to raise your personal vibrations so they become more in tune with the angels. Thus, one of the first things you must do is to understand why you should purify not just yourself but also the environment in which you exist. The best recommendation is to take a Reiki attunement course for you to better align with the Angels and their ways. Once you have cleared away the toxic emotions you will not only feel better in yourself, you will also begin to attract a better way of life based on how you now view the truth and integrity within the new vibrations you are now experiencing.

You will begin to see angels exist in a world of subtle energy while we ordinary folk live on the physical plane with our five senses. The angels are naturally attracted to people who not only have these higher states of consciousness they also note those prepared to improve their way of life and enjoy their new and much more healthy lifestyles.

Because of the many changes and sacrifices I made in my early life I must also have changed physically as well. Quite a few friends and acquaintances have failed to recognise me for they have said so when we meet including my mother at one time. Many people I used to know seem to have faded out of my life as the years have slipped. Some used to sap my energies and were not a loss as such for I felt dragged down almost as if I were a sponge soaking up their negativity and harmful ways. (When in such a harsh environment one should call on the Archangel Michael for protection.) People tend to stay away as you progress along such a path which is really rather hard at first but then the rewards are so uplifting as we draw like minded souls into our orbit such pain eases immensely.

The expectation that everyone is or can be loving and light is not a reality at all. You see, I had grown so many wings I had lost the ability to understand lower thought patterns or thinking. The dense energy of the earth plane had become a difficult place for me to be in. I had often thought of home and wanting to be there for I seemed to be always affirming the positive which resulted in most people looking at me as though I were from another planet.

I could see that my work here was to help shift the lower frequency of people to that of light and love and to help them see the bright side of things, not the dark sabotaging thoughts that had taken them over. So, obviously I had a major task on my hands but I was beginning to see positive results and that was a good thing. People would move away from me feeling more empowered with more positive thinking. I was getting great feedback because after all, if we manage to receive back a little hope then this can and will help move many mountains.

My life became much more sheltered and I found myself living in what seemed to be a permanent bubble. Even my husband used to say to me that I was living in my own world and, on reflection, I suppose I was. However, I couldn't be around people who were consistently complaining and moaning about life in general. As an employed person I found working with others hard for this took away my choice of with whom I might share my time.

In these modern times most people appear to be for ever stuck with miserable life-sucking jobs that drain quite a bit from their inner energies. Relationships often seem to be full of resentment and anger; for them life is harsh. As a healer I am able to see the situation from a higher perspective and help people move to a more harmonious existence.

But some folk don't want to change almost alike the old saying that you can lead a horse to water but you can't make it drink. We all have the potential to create a better way of life but it has to start with you and when we take on this responsibility we empower ourselves to create harmony in most areas of our life. Probably because one way or another most of us live in world of clutter of all kinds, we really do need to clear things out of the way in order to pursue a much better way of life

To properly de-clutter the way we exist, a quite hard task at the best of times, we need to not only make the effort but it has to be a worthwhile project as well. So, for those who would be interested, choose a time and or a day where you can and will be quite impartial and start in your home.

Clear away out all the belongings and bits and pieces you no longer need or use. Turn them over to your local charity shop – they will be so pleased with whatever you give them. The next phase is to clean up – but properly. This means a mop, a brush and a duster and polish. Set to and clean everywhere – thoroughly. While you are at it, do make sure you clean the windows as well and leave them open afterwards. In other words, really let the fresh air in. Light a candle or two and let them waft their beautiful perfumes all round the home and, while you are at it, play some soft music in the background.

It doesn't matter if you have never tried it before but why not buy a few crystals locally and place them to help cleanse and improve the energies in your home. Your local stockist will willingly advise you about the right ones to start with and when this is all achieved have a look around to check to see if there are any objects that are now less attractive - like they once were perhaps. Of course, don't just stop at the home - have a look in your wardrobe next and see about all the older clothing or items you bought but didn't like and take them to the charity shop.

This type of cleansing will have an effect on your psyche and you will, eventually, be glad you that did it for when we do have a clear out we make room for something new. Any emptiness will be replaced with the newer energy that now enters your life.

There are some people who feel tempted to become vegetarian or cut down on their meat and fish intake. I did, and have not looked back. But not everyone can manage this extremely radical change in their pattern of life. In addition to this you may not be aware of just how negative the news and media people can be by their constant broadcasting or printing the bad news. Try to draw away from too heavy a diet of this material and you will soon begin to get to feel so much better within yourself.

As this is the principal aim you cannot help but to feel better about so many other things – and people, as well.

CHAPTER FIFTEEN

Deciphering The Wheat From The Chaff

WHEN PEOPLE START OUT WITH a curious mind about spiritual matters they tend to feel tempted to try to connect with the spirit world in rather the same ways that other mediums and clairvoyants do – a connection to the higher self! This is good and strongly recommended but with exception to those who are mentally ill either temporarily or permanently.

I was not actively seeking at the time and it just happened to me. I was visited several times by spirit and so at this point I am taking the opportunity to encourage others to take their first steps along their spiritual pathways. The majority of people usually find their way to where a circle is being held and sit in with both professionals and those who have the gift and develop along the available lines in that fashion. In my own development much of the time was spent in my own environment.

After all of the experiences I have had I decided that I wanted to keep my work specific and with the angels only for I preferred to work their protective and positive energy. This is not to say that I do not receive messages from loved ones who have passed on.

Where possible I will always pass on the message to the person with me at the time for I realise how much comfort this may bring. The spirit world has orchestrated their visit most of the time anyway so all I have to do is channel it properly. For me this has been about rising up to a higher level and working with the angels for healing both people and animals.

The spirit world is rather a complex subject to fully understand so, simply put, it is my belief that when we leave our physical body we pass on to another dimension. How far along the system we may be allowed to pass will depend on how evolved we may have become while still on the earthly plane. If we were a spiritual person we would almost certainly ascend much higher than if we were more of a non-spiritual person.

Some spirits seem to prefer to stay close to this earthly plane and may appear to haunt certain places. There is a fair amount of evidence for this and I have witnessed much of this for myself. Once in the spirit world the new entrant can appear to become unable to pass successfully to the other side. Further and similar to Sam's story (chapter 7), I also believe that there may be other life forms along with we humans out there – but this is a subject of much debate.

When we are receptive or "open" it is possible that "lower entities" can and do attach themselves to us but, unfortunately, many are unaware that they are open. This may lead a small handful of people to be wrongly labelled as having a mental illness or suffering from a psychosis of some kind. Of course, I am not suggesting that these people are ignorant of the spiritual world but some of them may receive messages but be unable to process them for they are "open" but quite unable to do anything about it.

In some case messages from a lower energy force may be quite harsh and probably quite demanding. One might experience a small element of fear and feel a tad queasy in their solar plexus region. This is because lower energy entities enjoy making you feel off-balance because it feeds on this feeling of fear. The higher energy beings are more positive and loving; you should feel warm and have a sense of ease surround you. Body wisdom is very intelligent and manages to decipher such messages rather cleverly and somehow let you know that what you are receiving is right or wrong.

Once you have developed a sense of spirit and are able to become "open" to messages you should be able to elevate yourself in such a way as to be able to call up the spirits and ask for help and guidance with whatever may be troubling you at the time. This takes time and requires you to become reasonably familiar and trusting with those whom you seek. Once this angel "awareness" has come about you will become far more receptive and open to the guidance offered. Your angel friends are just waiting for your permission to be of assistance when you ask for their help.

We all have an aura - the energy field that surrounds us. The aura may be considered as a multi layered subtle energy field that is always around our physical body but is not always seen by ordinary folk at the best of times. People who are sensitive often see or sense this aura and will tell you if there are any weaknesses in any of the seven basic layers that make up the whole.

These seven layers are comprised of the physical auric body, the etheric auric body, the vital auric body, the astral auric body, the lower mental auric body, the higher mental auric body and the spiritual auric body. When the aura becomes dirtied through negative thought patterns or old memories the angels will not be able to connect with you properly. This is largely a warning not to overdo smoking, drinking or drugs or allow past negative events cloud the memory too much for this can and does affect the aura.

As long as you look after your health and enjoy positive thoughts your aura will remain strong because it needs to be properly grounded. At any time negative thinking or events are always far better handled by a healthy aura whereas negative issues of any kind will be rejected as long as you stay this way.

There are several ways of cleansing the aura. Close your eyes and try to visualise the aura that surrounds your body and you will begin to see colours. They will be very pale at first but as time passes and you become more proficient in this exercise and colours will be detected.

Try to imagine that your aura is being cleaned by a white light above your head rather like a shower cascading down to the floor. Allow this to continue on until you feel that you should stop. Set aside a time and place to perform this every day. For most people this would be at night and in the early morning when you are less likely to be disturbed.

The aura is composed of many colours and each is assigned a meaning in terms of how you should be feeling. When grey is the overall shade you may be feeling low and may be slightly depressed. Worries are causing you to feel low. When white predominates you should be feeling relaxed expanded, happy and in touch with your clear and happy higher self.

If the overall hue is of a turquoise shade then you will have clarity and easy communication. There will also be a state of feeling calm and compassionate. Green implies a calm and focused state there will be an aura of love around you – a healing energy with a loving nature. If purple is the strongest shade you will be very much connected to and with your higher self and there will be a sense of heightened sensitivity. Your psychic abilities will be sharper. Yellow suggests a perceptive state of intelligence. You will be happy within yourself, full of joy, creative and optimistic

When red is the dominant shade you will be frustrated and angry because you don't feel grounded. There should be plenty of energy and you'll feel quite focused. Orange almost always implies a sense of creativity. Your sense of fair play will be strong. You will be playful and driven. Shades of pink always refer to a loving, friendly nature; you will be artistic, sensitive and thoughtful. Whenever blue is the strongest hue you will be protective, talkative, sensitive and truthful.

When violet tops the colours the suggestion is of a visionary outlook and you will feel quite intuitive as well as idealistic, caring and compassionate. Black almost always implies sadness, grief even and there may be a strong sense of draining or a fear you may not understand. Indigo may be interpreted as being an above average sensitivity along with very deep thoughts.

Silver suggests an abundance of ability an awakening with a stronger sense of receptiveness. Gold always means a high sense of spiritual integrity that makes you very clear seeing. Finally, but just as often nevertheless, when you sense a collection of hues and shades that you feel surrounded by a rainbow of colours your intuitive nature will be clear and most enlightened.

Remember, your aura is important and it must be kept pure and unsullied at all times because when you receive messages from the spirit world the angels will become known to you through the colours you will see in the aura of the other person who is with you at the time.

To be ready to meet your own angel you should set aside a time and place to communicate. Create a period of patience and calm for this will help to make the link between you quite strong. This is what I call my "coffee time" with them and when I can really relax and just let myself be. I spend most days with my angel and just become connected to share and treat her like I would a best friend. The more time you share together the stronger the link will become and you will see how much you grow as a person when you tap into their divine wisdom.

It is very important that you become aware of the names of the angels who come to connect and bond with you at these special times. It will work both ways for no matter who we are we do like the sound of our name when others call us – for whatever purpose.

To make this a sacred connection your guardian angel is always with you ready to help with compassion and clear guidance. He or she will love and support you when you ask and all you have to do is ask. However, you must first ensure that you will not be disturbed so remember to switch off the home phone and your mobile as well. It really is surprising how many people forget to do this.

Light a candle and make yourself comfortable preferably sitting up in a comfortable chair. A little music won't hurt as long as it soft and gentle. A few flowers are nice for they make a lot of difference to a connection because your room has some energy in it and you need to be able to raise the quantity and the quality of whatever may be there.

Try to imagine that there are cords stretching downward from your feet into the earth. Now reverse the idea so that you feel the cords are now moving upward back toward to your feet, through your chakras and on and upward into the greater universe where it will meet a large mass of white light.

Now envisage the cord attach to this white light after which it will begin to pull the light down towards you through your chakras and down again through your feet to the earth. Now think of a golden egg hovering over you but that the higher "you" is inside the egg. Silently ask of your angel to step into your aura and make him- or herself known to you. You may feel a tingling sensation, or perhaps think that your hair is being touched softly. There will be a change of pressure now and a name will enter into you mind.

The angels will almost always make you feel that a great love surrounds you and it's about now that you may ask the presence for his or her name then quietly await a response. Use the first name you that comes into your mind. Next, you may now feel free to ask of your angel for their help with whatever problem for which you are seeking advice.

You can repeat your query re the angel's name and ask for a sign to be given – it won't hurt if this takes a few days. Now you may politely ask for the connection to stop and for the angel to withdraw their energy from yours.

It is safe now to open your eyes and be ready to take in the signs that may come to you over the next few days or so. As you start to come back to normal awareness always remember to thank the angel for their help.

It would be rather nice if you could always use this same small area each time you practice to connect with your guide or guides. You only need a small space to turn into a sanctuary like area and, preferable, a place where no one else may venture when it is not in use.

CHAPTER SIXTEEN
Angelic Reiki Healing And The Angels

THIS SYSTEM OF HEALING WAS created by Kevin Core and Christine DeHeera; it was channelled to Kevin from the Archangel Metatron and Dwul khul in 2002. It helps to awaken you to your soul energy and, having experienced this I can personally vouch for the whole concept.

My healing career began in 2001 when I was attuned to Tera Mai Seichem Healing which is founded in Egyptian teachings having been created by Kathryn Milner who lives in the United States of America. I could not believe how such wonderful methods could make such difference to a life until I experienced it for myself.

I recommend one should try an healing attunment, that is of course, always assuming you are prepared embrace a new you; a new way of existing in this world, of being ready to step upward to your Ascension Pathway,

This is not for the faint hearted. It means personal growth and moving beyond your present "ego self" to embrace the higher purpose for you here and in this life time. Having taken part in this I can honestly say that I have had many challenges along with much joy since I became a healer.

There are a wide variety of experiences for one to learn and to become accustomed while living on this plane.

To begin with you will have to clear away old patterns and, as you proceed you will become more sensitive to spirit, as you make a better connection with your soul you also learn how to be more compassionate and, of course, your healing power develops more strongly. You develop a happier and more blissful transformation of your old self. Ties to the past are released and the feeling of personal "one-ness" is apparent as you begin your ascension.

Angelic Reiki is similar to other Reiki Attunement and uses similar symbols but the Archangel Metatron channelled a newer, fresher version to Kevin Core and they are very powerful. Another difference with angelic Reiki is that the angels supervise the attunement themselves. We in turn then channel it to other recipients.

During the course of my first attunement I seemed to develop powerful visions of an energy vortex spinning in front of me. Through my chakras it felt surreal and after I was cleared of a major block in my life I was very grateful. Since practising this new method I have developed much more clarity of vision and understanding. I have been given what could be termed a system of "X-ray vision" in order that I may see more clearly into the inner workings of the body of a client to help them. People who have had this experienced have all felt an amazing difference for the energy transference seems so much purer.

The healing channel develops in a much better and clearer way. There is more openness after this method is employed. This was proved one day as I was sitting next to another young lady along with some three or four others. She suddenly complained of a painful arm in that she felt unable to move it properly. I remember that I touched her shoulder lightly where the pain was and then gently rubbed it. Apparently her pain disappeared so quickly she looked at me almost unbelievingly wondering where the pain had gone.

Absent Healing is also very powerful and I have seen so many benefits in its use. We are able to send this kind of healing with the intention to heal a person wherever they may be at the time. We envisage where they are, their trouble and try to imagine them in front of us. We then hold that picture in our mind's eye and wait for what we do to have an effect.

I remember once that my sister was going through a difficult patch and was aware that she needed healing so I enquired of her higher self for permission to help. After the healing in a healing chapel surrounded by angels and without her being aware she claimed she felt like a new person. She added that she did not know why she felt such a difference – just rather pleased that all the heaviness had been lifted away.

The Spirit will always put us in the right place at the right time and bring people to us who need healing. People with such psychic powers are here to heal and are guided by their inner "knowing" from source to either write or conduct energy healing, lecture, counsel, or be useful in other ways.

I have always followed my guide which is why I do this work now. It is my soul's journey to heal but before I arrived at my present stage I had to heal and clean myself. This involved a lot of soul searching and letting go of my old way of existing. Clairvoyance serves me in such a way that I can see the real story behind the mask that most people wear. I can now "see" the soul and why it is going through what is happening to it. Then I help to unravel it all but always with the client's highest good in my mind and heart.

If or when you should ever feel a calling to work as a healer always accept it because it is so very rewarding. You will know that your angels will guide you to the people and places to study this new chosen healing life you adopt and sooner or later doors will open for you quite effortlessly. You are likely to be guided to all types of healing and don't worry, for you will know somehow as to which is the right or wrong way for you. Indeed, one should always listen to that inner voice for it will never fail you.

Perhaps the most important thing for you to remember is that you owe it to yourself as well as to your client that you must always be a clear channel for the best healing. You have to take the responsibility for your wellbeing at all levels. I would only take healing from someone who was grounded and healthy and who had been practising for some time many years. After all, we all want the best so it advisable to set your set your intentions as high as you can at all times. .

Try to meditate every day to clear your chakras and learn to enjoy the experience. There are two principal reasons for this. You will want to be calm and serene at all times and there will be a need to connect with your guide or guides so that will be able to fully understand the messages with more clarity

A still and peaceful mind is a happy one – far different form the busy one you may have had in earlier days.

CHAPTER SEVENTEEN

Spirit Release

For me Spirit Release is a sensitive subject having experienced first-hand as a Healer, attachments and possession, when I thought I was going crazy in my younger years all the time, I found out the reason and got the appropriate help and I was happy for that help. There are so many resources available to us nowadays regarding Spirit Attachment you can even train at a college to work as a Release Therapist.

So times are changing as it is becoming more acceptable to talk about this subject.

Spiritual Churches are a great place to go to learn from other Healers and Mediums, they work with spirit all the time on different levels, my advice would be to listen to your own intuition and follow that.

What does it feel like to have an attachment?

You will simply not be yourself, you may feel something on your body, and behave in a different way, and you may feel spaced out or not at home.

You may get depressed and withdraw from the world it could be a number of things and you will be able to tell and know you are not yourself, You may be behaving in a way that the person attached to you may of behaved when they were alive, let's say they were into betting you may want to go to betting shops or read the pages on a betting form in a newspaper all of a sudden! And some other symptoms are:-

Sudden change in behaviour
Fear and phobias you didn't have before set in
Sudden cravings
Thoughts of Suicide
This is an example of the attachments hold over you.

These Discarnate spirits become lossed souls between two worlds, trapped here on the Earth plane wandering around causing havoc and looking for a host, which could help them feel they are alive again, its like plugging into a battery source for energy and your Aura is perfect for that, eventually manipulating you into doing the things they enjoyed whilst alive like smoking etc, they can become devious and try to hide within you and may feel you are going mad, some people end up in psychiatric hospitals because their behaviour becomes unrecognisable to them and there families.

I have experienced such events and am here to tell the tale and thus help others to understand what is happening to them.

If you feel different keep a journal and see what you are experiencing on a daily basis this is a good starting point, notice if you get voices that are not your own, don't worry you won't be psychotic it is how the spirit of the person is communicating with you, some people get really worried at this point

As I did years ago.... but when you know what it is and who!, you can then be stronger to move it on and protect yourself.

Spirits will normally attach themselves to people who are vulnerable and open.

We are not all aware of that vulnerability until it is too late.

Some of the symptoms of vulnerability are:-

No sense of Space for self

Tired and lethargic

Depression

Insomnia

Feelings of Helplessness

Chronic Fatigue

Is your Aura Strong?

As mentioned in a previous chapter your Aura is your coating of amour it is what we have to protect us and inform us of subtle changes, on a psychic level, your aura is like your antenna on the radio

It picks up and receives information and then deciphers it.

If you Aura is damaged it will let negative in including spirits, we are subectible when we are at our lowest, or in ill health this is when we can attract lower entities and thought forms that can attack us

Some of the attacking can be done from your own Psyche, when you constantly mull over and over about something or someone whom has hurt you or done you wrong.

But if the thought's are not yours you will able to tell!, this is when we start to get worried and need to protect ourselves.

So how do you move them on?

So if you feel you have an attachment you need to act on it to get it removed before it does any damage.

You can go and see a speaclist in this area.

What occurs is the therapist will relax you and then they will start to communicate with the spirit by using your fingers as an answer from the attachment/spirit. I.e. move this finger for yes and vice versa.

When this has taken place the therapist will ask the spirit to leave and invite in a door keeper to do so.

And take them away a simple but powerful process, this is practised by a lady called * **Susan Allen** who teaches at The School of Psychic Studies.

Another method I use is the Dowsing Method, I will dowse the person first to see where the Attachment is I will ask what the sex of this person is and get more information from the pendulum

Then I go to a healing Temple in meditation and I stand the person before a circle of Angels

We send Healing to the person with the Attachment.

I call in Archangel Zadkeil to work with me we send beams of Light to the person.

Then we move closer and closer and we lift off the Attachment together and it is removed and taken away, then quickly replaced with a new aura and shield.

If you have no experience in this area, which not many people do!, I would recommend seeing a specialist first, the chances are the spirit will be wise to you catching on, and will try to hide its self they can be very devious, so caution is warranted when you find out.

I know this all sound a bit wacky and way out, but I have done this on people and they are a different person after.

There are many article's available on the internet regarding this subject, my advice would be to keep an open mind and not dismiss anything until you journal and step back and observe yourself if in doubt act.

CHAPTER EIGHTEEN

How To Protect Yourself And Knowing Why

PSYCHIC AND SPIRITUAL PROTECTION IS not just about esoteric matters it is also about the living people around us and how they affect our lives by the energy they give off when around us. Some people attract others towards them by their kind energy and giving ways but this can be harmful if the people are "toxic" or dysfunctional in any way for they feed from your positive energy and that leaves you feeling tired and drained almost as if the life force has gradually been syphoned from you.

To a certain extent people can be helped for we can give them the tools to change but the responsibility rests with them ultimately. As a healer I have had many times when people have called me at all times of the day for assistance. So far, I have been able to show them how to change the type of thinking that has bought them thus far to this place.

If you have not established good healthy boundaries you will feel totally drained and be weakened by all of this. Empathy and compassion become natural strong points within us and to this end we want to help others but without these boundaries in place it really is a most difficult task.

Perhaps the following case scenario will illustrate what I mean.

Clair came to see me on many occasions because she was feeling weak and helpless regarding a decision she felt she needed to make about her life. However, she seemed to keep playing the victim so asked for help with making a decision she was unsure of the changes she was facing and felt that she had to have someone give her permission to move forward. She felt that by getting approval to make such a choice that it would take decision out of her hands. If it all went wrong she could blame someone else for her bad choice.

I asked her to make a choice based on trust and not fear and to see what would happen. But she never did this and seemed to be just running around in circles for some time and still hurting all the while. When she visited me I would make sure I kept to a strict time code for she knew nothing about boundaries because her own were weak. I asked her to have faith and to ask her higher self what it would do to help her, to which she replied it would remove the fear from her.

Eventually she made a choice. This empowered herself to become strong and she began to listen to herself more and more. It was as though she took back her personal responsibility and, of course, by doing so she became happier in herself as a result.

When Clair came to physically visit me or just call me on the telephone I had to position protection and boundaries around me because of the lack of her own boundaries. Her negative self-talk was so draining that even though I wanted to help her I first had to be in a position to do so properly because when we are clear and focused in ourselves we also assume the responsibility for ourselves in respect of our mental, physical and spiritual well-being.

With good emotional health we love ourselves more than anyone which is one of the first things we need to master to lead happy lives. Once this is established we have something to offer other people. Who we meet and who are need of help.

To become happy, strong and whole is not always easy for some folk if they have been abused through no fault of their own. However, despite this we can heal our lives with the tools available today. Among my favourite methods is hypnotherapy and Reiki for I believe we can see and make amazing strides with all that is available to us if we want to when we use these powers.

In respect of shielding and cleaning your personal energy levels one method is through a visualisation technique and is rather simple but very effective. To shield your energy from physical and psychic vampirism you have to try to imagine there is a white mist coming from the top of your head that cascades upward to about six inches above the crown. It then moves down and over the entire body to below the feet so you are completely enveloped in this white light. Of course, once you have arrived at this stage you must seal it.

Yet another method of ensuring safety and protection is through crystals. These minerals have been around for thousands of years. Although not fully understood by many they have been used in so many different ways to cure physical dis-ease and other ills and as remedies of just about all kinds they have proved invaluable for so many people.

Among some of these stones that have been and still are used for protection is Black Tourmaline which assists in neutralising psychic attack. Black Obsidian helps to repel and disperse negative thoughts. Amethyst is often employed against psychic attack and helps to strengthen the aura against negative energy attacks. One may also use Clear Quartz which is said to absorb and transmute negative energy into a much more positive state.

Another alternative system of protection that may be utilised to help keep you safe and well protected is through the use of affirmation. This is the saying and repeating of powerful positive words to bring about change: declaring and knowing that something is true or the practice of positive thinking.

An affirmation is a positive statement that describes a desired outcome. When repeated many times in order to impress the subconscious mind and trigger it into positive action it can be a most effective system of creating upward energy forces to work for you. If we say and visualise these words or phrase often enough we can change our behavioural patterns and ultimately change our way of life.

It is perfectly permissible to write them down as well as repeat them to yourself especially at first for this helps the message you are trying to get across sink in properly. In these troubled times so many of us think negatively that we are in danger of creating a downhill spiral of thoughts which can lead to misery and a lack of confidence. So, as you can see, there is a strong need to see ourselves achieve our dreams by doing something positive to bring about this state of idealistic thought and repeating an affirmation is yet another way of doing this. To talk to oneself using this inner dialogue of different affirmations means that you can choose the dialogue be it positive or negative for either will bring about what you want.

Negative thoughts are learned patterns from childhood. For example, if you were told you were stupid as a child you may grow up to believe that. This tends to have a negative effect on your life and you may have consciously or otherwise adopted some form of self-sabotage to prevent you from achieving what you really wanted.

Thus, every affirmation you make reflects the standard of the belief you have in in yourself.

Generally speaking the positive affirmation is a short but definite statement targeted at specific goals and life changing behaviour patterns. Affirmations do work although some folk tend not take too kindly to them as a rule. Such people seem to be unable to get their head around being positive. If you look at the media, especially where the news is concerned, there are almost always negative words that we note on a daily basis and which make it hard for us to be positive because we seem to exist in a world where bad news is a main diet – of fact or fiction.

We need to overcome this situation and the best way is to not let the negative approach of the media get to us. Our subconscious is mind is forced into seeing things differently and, eventually, it will cede to such methods. So, to help resist these pressures my advice would be to try a detox where the media is concerned for about a month or so. Without their daily negative input you will soon see how much more you can achieve.

Repeating affirmations will bring about a change in you and, hopefully, you will attract more positive things towards you. I'm not saying that you should become less interested in what is going on the world but I am saying that you must learn to decipher what is good for you and what is not.

Here are a few affirmations with their associated angels that I recommend. Remember to declare these in the present tense as if it already is done. Designate each day to one that is important and repeat the exercise a week later working through your most important ones.

The Angels that can help you with these Affirmations are the Archangel Michael, Maat and St Germain.

Suggested affirmations would be along the following lines.

For protection use, "I am always divinely protected." For love try, "I am loveable and happy in love." or, "I attract only healthy relationships." For health matters you could apply, "My body is healthy and I have lots of energy."

For more material concerns such as money you might use, "I have amazing prosperity and the more I have the more I can give. "I pay my bills easily and effortlessly." And for your self-esteem you could repeat, "I am my own unique self". I am OK." In terms of personal happiness try, "My heart sings daily with joy; life is wonderful and I am happy."

As far as friends and friendships are concerned you might say "I have the most amazing friends". I am blessed for my friends bring me happiness and love." Finally, in terms of peace you might try, "I choose peace every day. I trust in the process of life."

Of course, you can always make up your own affirmations which would be personal and very special to you. However, do remember, we can sabotage our approach to life with what we say so choose your words carefully. This is an exercise in personal self-protection first and foremost. You will soon learn to look after yourself with the affirmations you select for yourself.

CHAPTER NINETEEN

Archangel Metatron
Clear The Way

YOU MAY WANT TO RECORD this meditation before hand and then listen to it.

You find yourself at the foot of a large staircase- the stair case is gold

You are going to walk up the stairs 1 by 1......

Step 1 step -step 2-step 3 step 4- step 5-.........................step 15

You are facing a door way at the top of the stairs open the door and close it behind you

Enter a corridor and as you walk along the corridor sparkling lights pass by you brushing your Aura

The corridor is full of light the floor is polished white marble.

You approach another door this door is Gold. Open this door and walk forward and you find yourself in a golden pod shaped building this golden pod is protecting you and holding you safe

The pod is empty in the centre is a circle step forward and enter the circle stand here and wait,

The Archangel Metatron steps forward and joins you in this circle he is wearing a lovely robe shining brightly and it contains colours of the rainbow.

His face is soft and gentle as he smiles warmly at you. he points to a screen to your right-- a large white screen he then asks you to project your thoughts of what it is that is not working in your life due to lack of organisation, chaos and your unfocused attention- show him the areas that are concerning you on the screen everything to do with work and then home life, even relationships.

Archangel Metatron asks you now to project a clear beam of light onto the screen wiping away the chaos and making room for the new positive energy to enter.

On the screen place images of the new you and a clear image of how your life is now you are organised and focused, he empowers you to feel motivated instead of stuck

Driven instead of doubting yourself he propels you forward to the new life that awaits you.

Hold this image now for 2 minutes.

Next visualise a gold light entering your Crown on the top of your head, this is Archangel Metatrons energy he will guide you in the weeks and months ahead to help with any focus and attention that is needed, He sends the words to your mind FOCUS-ATTENTION-DISCAPLINE and you absorb them into
You consciousness.

You now see Metatron stand back and leave the circle, you thank him for his time.

You turn towards the door way and go back into the corridor closing the gold door behind you
And you walk down the corridor and still flecks of light and gold brush over you.

Open the door and see the staircase in front of you.

Step onto the top step and start to walk down each step 15-14-13-12-11-10-9-8-7-6-5-4-3-2-1
And when you are ready open your eyes.

About The Author

Jane McNally, BCMA, Itec Dip, ATP Ascet trained Teacher. Is a visionary, Angelic Reiki Master Teacher and Angel Teacher, she also is a psychic Medium and comes from a 3rd Generation of Psychics.

Jane has had a interest in the Paranormal since she was young after seeing spirit at home she was curious to find out more, after having many paranormal experiences the realization of her gift and sensitivity made her follow the prompts from the Angels/Ascended Masters and spirit guides and since then has trained as a therapist and teacher, her work involves workshops and seminars and training others to become healers.

She has been on Sky TV regularly as a presenter and reader and appeared in spiritual magazines such as "take a break fate and fortune magazine."

Jane has helped thousands of people globally with her Healing and Messages from Angels. She has testimonials to be proud of.

Website www.the-angels-within.co.uk